GARDEN CITIES OF TO-MORROW

THE MIT PAPERBACK SERIES

GARDEN CITIES OF TO-MORROW

by

EBENEZER HOWARD

Edited, with a Preface, by

F. J. OSBORN

With an Introductory Essay by

LEWIS MUMFORD

THE M.I.T. PRESS

Massachusetts Institute of Technology

Cambridge, Massachusetts

Published in Great Britain by
Faber and Faber Ltd
First M.I.T. Press Paperback Edition, February, 1965

Library of Congress Catalog Card Number: 65-10521
Printed in Great Britain

Contents

DIAGRAMS AND PLANS

Foreword to this Edition

Since the 1946 edition of this book there have been great advances in planning thought, legislation and practice. The two prefaces of that date, now reprinted without revision (except for a change in the footnote on page 13), must therefore be read, along with Howard's text of 1898, in historical perspective. It is possible in this edition to add only the following brief note on what has happened since 1946.

Under the New Towns Act of that year about twenty new towns, essentially conforming to Howard's Garden City definition, have been founded in Great Britain. Those now nearing completion have proved remarkably successful as places to live in and efficient centres of modern industry. Moreover, taken together they more than pay their way as national investments. They have aroused intense interest throughout the world as demonstrations of the practicability of the relief of congestion in overgrown cities by some planned dispersal of people and workplaces to new towns beyond reserved green belts, thereby permitting central renewal on more spacious and humane standards.

Town planning has become a major governmental function, and is broadening out to regional and national planning. Among the many problems it faces is that of the control or guidance of the location of industry, and of office businesses, in order to bring about a healthier, more pleasant, and more efficient distribution of people and their activities in town and country. The fear of a declining population mentioned in Lewis Mumford's preface has been replaced by the prospect of an embarrassingly rapid increase, which magnifies the necessity for new towns. Indeed this, and almost all the other changes in society and thought since 1898, confirm the validity of Howard's thesis.

The book list in the 1946 edition remains of value for those interested in the early history of the Garden City movement.

A few of the older books have now been replaced by a selection from the copious flow of recent publications that will help to bring the reader up to date. Some of these contain more ample bibliographies.

January, 1965.   F. J. O.

Preface by F. J. Osborn

Ebenezer Howard's book was first published in 1898 as *To-morrow: a Peaceful Path to Real Reform*, and re-issued with slight revisions in 1902 under the title *Garden Cities of To-morrow*. The present edition follows the 1902 text, except that I have reinstated from the 1898 edition a few of Howard's quotations from other writers that seem to me to have new interest to-day. The diagrams I have included in their 1902 form. Though their style seems antiquated by contrast with the living freshness of Howard's writing, they are an integral part of the book, and having been drawn by Howard himself they tell us something of his practical yet non-technical constructiveness and his gifts of popular persuasion.

The history of the book and its effects is full of paradoxes. It endowed all modern languages with a new term (*Garden City*, *Cité-Jardin*, *Gartenstadt*, *Cuidad-jardín*, *Tuinstad*), and though this term was given a most precise meaning by Howard, everywhere it has been used persistently in a sense entirely different from, indeed opposed to, the author's definition.

Again, the book holds a unique place in town planning literature, is cited in all planning bibliographies, stands on the shelves of the more important libraries, and is alluded to in most books on planning; yet most of the popular writers on planning do not seem to have read it—or if they have read it, to remember what it says.

Further, the book led to two experiments in town-founding which by imitation, and imitation of imitation, have had immeasurable influence on practical urban development throughout the world. Parallel with but largely independently of these developments, the book set going ideas which, after a long interval, have transformed the scientific and political outlook on town structure and town growth. Yet no book of significance has enjoyed less academic notice or prestige. With the exception of Alfred Marshall and Charles Gide no economist of the first rank has, until the last few years, seriously entertained Howard's central idea that the size of towns is a proper subject of conscious control. Of the recognized formative writers on town planning only Sir Raymond Unwin fully understood that idea; and it is a subsidiary paradox that, as Mr. Lewis Mumford says, Unwin's life-work (after his part in the planning of the First Garden City at Letchworth) did in fact crystallize the pattern of the universal suburban developments of which, as a disciple of Howard, he disapproved in principle. As to the sociologists, it has taken them forty years of data-collecting and subtle analysis to arrive at the stage of focusing on the size of geographical community units as a major factor in social organization, all of them (except Patrick Geddes and Mr. Mumford) studiously ignoring Howard's work in the process.

The reason for this academic neglect is not far to seek. Howard did not seem a 'scientific' writer; his book avoids technical terminology, displays no great learning, contains little historical or demographic documentation. Neither did it become a bestseller exercising that massive effect on popular attitudes which students of social affairs are reluctantly compelled to respect. Yet it is surprising to me that so few trained thinkers detected that Howard possessed extraordinary intuition and judgment; that he had descried and fastened upon a neglected problem of major social importance; and that in his chosen field he had a shrewd instinct for discriminating the permanently significant from the ephemeral in the ideas of his time. It is not to be denied that in this book he made far-reaching assumptions which a cautious student would not immediately accept, and that he made no attempt to substantiate them by a parade of authorities and statistics. But his assumptions were in fact almost wholly right, because they were based on a wide sympathy with the habits and desires of common people. It was by unselfconscious common sense and humane understanding, rather than by systematic fact-finding and analysis, that Howard got to the heart of the urban problem.

Though it is the special problem of city structure to which the book is addressed, and upon which its contribution is of historic importance, a reader of to-day cannot but be interested in what it implies as to changes in the political background. Seeing that nearly half a century has passed since Howard wrote, it is astonishing how pertinent his thought is to our current controversies. He foresaw the vast extension of municipal enterprise. But unlike the numerous community-theorists who preceded him, he did not project this principle to infinity. He was as much concerned for free enterprise as for social control; and his experimental attitude and tentative suggestions as to the boundary between the two, as to devolution of democratic control, and as to the sphere of voluntary co-operation, are relevant to our present situation. More remarkable still, his conception of town planning as team-work and as a fluid process ('this plan, or if the reader be pleased so to term it, this absence of plan'), is just the conception we are now arriving at after decades of narrow ideas of planning and even narrower resistances to planning. The book contains many such flashes of foresight. But when it appeared, it seems to have struck the conservative-minded as merely fantastic, and idealists of the political Left as disrespectful to their over-simplified panaceas. Even some of the realistic reformers of the Fabian Society dismissed Howard's scheme as futile and impracticable.[1]

Thus it came about that the influence of this book on the wider world of thought was not direct, but through the results of its impact on the minds of a handful of energetic and capable men who experimented in practical town development. The lesser things these men did were copied in detail all over the world. Their greater achievement, which derived from Howard's proposals, was never more than dimly understood. The meaning

[1] 'His plans would have been in time if they had been submitted to the Romans when they conquered Britain. They set about laying-out cities, and our forefathers have dwelt in them to this day. Now Mr. Howard proposes to pull them all down and substitute garden cities, each duly built according to pretty coloured plans, nicely designed with a ruler and compass. The author has read many learned and interesting writers, and the extracts he makes from their books are like plums in the unpalatable dough of his Utopian scheming. We have got to make the best of our existing cities, and proposals for building new ones are about as useful as would be arrangements for protection against visits from Mr. Wells's Martians.'—*Fabian News* Dec. 1898.

and the vital importance of the Garden City idea became obscured, almost lost, in the process.

Yet for a year or two after the publication of *To-morrow* the project of building new manufacturing towns in the long-settled land of Britain attracted immense popular interest. Howard lectured on the subject all over the country, and in 1899, having collected a number of enthusiasts, he formed the Garden City Association. By 1901 he was reinforced by the adherence of the late Ralph Neville, K.C. (afterwards Mr. Justice Neville) who became chairman of the Association and brought much practical wisdom to its campaign, the late Thomas Adams (afterwards the well-known consultant town planner) who became secretary, and an able and influential group of manufacturers and men prominent in public life. General scepticism prevailed as to whether a project so novel and daring could be translated into fact; but the group proved to have the standing, the ability and the idealism to do it. A Pioneer Company was registered, and in 1903, after much investigation, a rural site of 3,818 acres was purchased by private treaty in Hertfordshire, thirty-five miles from central London, and the First Garden City of Letchworth was initiated.

The story of the establishment of Letchworth has been told elsewhere,[1] and I will not repeat it here. The judgment of the able group of business men who started the town was nowhere better shown than in their choice of the then unknown architects Raymond Unwin and Barry Parker to prepare the town plan. Unwin, a man of great technical ability, immediately grasped the significance of Howard's ideas, and like Howard himself he was alert to the emerging social forces and popular aspirations that were to transform housing and factory design in the next generation. Later, as the draftsman of the Tudor-Walters Housing Report (1918), he was to establish the modern house-and-garden standard that characterized the vast British building effort of the inter-war years. There were anticipations of that standard at Bournville and elsewhere; but Letchworth played the most conspicuous part in demonstrating its popularity. The foundation of Garden City Associations in many

[1] The best account is in C. B. Purdom's *Building of Satellite Towns* (1949).

other countries, and of the International Garden City Association (afterwards the International Housing and Town Planning Federation), with Howard as its President, gave Letchworth world-wide fame; the town became the Mecca of housing and planning reformers from every country; and it was not the fault of its founders that experts concentrated more and more interest on the Letchworth housing standard and the minutiae of its lay-out, and less and less on the larger idea it was built to illustrate.

For Letchworth was, and remains, a faithful fulfilment of Howard's essential ideas. It has to-day a wide range of prosperous industries, it is a town of homes and gardens with ample open spaces and a spirited community life, virtually all its people find their employment locally, it is girdled by an inviolate agricultural belt, and the principles of single ownership, limited profit, and the earmarking of any surplus revenue for the benefit of the town have been fully maintained. The permitted maximum dividend on the share capital has been declared for many years, though some arrears from the early stages of construction remain to be paid off[1]. Commercially the venture has been as successful as a first essay in a new field could have been expected to be. From the wider standpoint of national finance it is a triumphantly economic proposition—the housing subsidies per head it has had from the state being negligible by comparison with those poured out for intensive development in the older cities. Its health record is better than that of any other industrial town except the Second Garden City at Welwyn. As a proof of the practicability of establishing an entirely new detached industrial community on a virgin site, Letchworth's success is unquestionable. Of no less importance is its demonstration of the technique of organic town planning under the system of unified estate ownership and leasehold, and the compatibility of that system with the freedom of industrial and business enterprises and the democratic conduct of a town's affairs.

Of Welwyn Garden City, which was the result of Howard's personal initiative in 1919, I need say little. Its contribution to

[1]Arrears were paid in 1946; in 1956 the dividend limit was abandoned, but under the Letchworth Garden City Corporation Act of 1962 the estate became public property in 1963.

Garden City history is that it carried further than Letchworth the technique of civic design and architectural harmony, and in the organization of its shopping centre and factory area it conducted interesting experiments which merit careful study by all who are concerned with the economics of large-scale development. Being nearer London than Letchworth, it has a more appreciable proportion of residents who travel daily in to the Metropolis, but at least 85 per cent of its working population find their employment in the town, which has a wide variety of industries and some large commercial office businesses—a class of enterprise now found to be more susceptible of dispersal than has been hitherto supposed.[1]

The establishment of Letchworth did not lead to the widespread foundation of new towns on the same principle, anticipated by Howard in Chapter XII of this book. It is worth while to ponder on this. Since 1898 the population of Great Britain has increased by eleven millions, and the number of its dwellings by four to five millions. It is certain that new factories and community buildings have been built in like proportions. In other words, we have added to our stock of buildings in that period the equivalent of at least 300 towns on Howard's formula. Yet we have only two garden cities, with a combined population of less than 40,000.

Where have these extra millions of people and dwellings been placed in the meantime? Mostly in the vastly expanded suburbs of our cities. Greater London alone—the continuously built-up Metropolitan area—has added two and a quarter millions to its population since Howard wrote his book. There has been some reduction of the numbers living in the central wards of the cities, due to the migration of better-off families to the suburbs. But this has not reduced congestion much, if at all, because business premises in the centres have very greatly expanded, and have encroached on land formerly occupied by dwellings. Owing to the decline in the birth-rate, families have become smaller; the number of families, or households, per acre of the central residential districts, in British cities, has probably increased rather than diminished. In many American cities, on

[1] See *Dispersal*: an Enquiry made by the National Council of Social Service (1944).

the other hand, the suburban migration has resulted in the virtual abandonment of extensive inner areas.

The publication of Howard's book was coincident with the first experiments in electric traction, of which he saw the possibilities, and with the beginnings of the petrol or gasoline motor, which he does not mention. These new forms of transport, which could have been used to bring about the pattern of 'Social Cities' he described, were used instead to facilitate the sprawling of suburbs, a type of urban growth wasteful from the economic standpoint and disadvantageous socially. Coupled with the rise of real incomes, rapid transport has enabled the people moving out from the centres to find the open residential surroundings they desired. But they and the numerous inmigrants from rural areas have obtained these surroundings at the expense of long and costly daily journeys to and from work. Local community life has been weakened or destroyed, and access to the country made more difficult for the large numbers of residents still left in city centres.

There has certainly been much 'decentralization' of industry in the period; but industrial firms, seeking space, light and cheap land, have with few exceptions settled themselves in or near the suburban fringes of the larger population centres, for reasons that show little imaginative foresight but are easily understandable. On the other hand commercial and service businesses, which have grown far more rapidly than manufacturing industry, have for reasons equally understandable and uninspired, expanded enormously in the city centres, their skyscrapers and monumental blocks accounting for most of the rebuilding that has occurred in these centres and of the increase of employment therein. Relatively little rebuilding of dwellings has been done in the inner parts of cities; some bad slum areas have been cleared, a proportion of their displaced occupiers rehoused at great public expense in tenement flats, and old middle-class houses sub-divided for citizens who lack the means, the time or the enterprise to make the 'happy journey' to the suburbs.

By tacit co-operation (conspiracy is an unfair word for so mentally supine a process) public policy has supported private enterprise, in business location, transport, and building, in fostering this form of city development. Any attempt to break from it by one of the participating agencies would have seemed risky or impracticable. A change of the direction of growth would certainly have needed some degree of co-ordination, but such a change was never even seriously entertained. This is the story of British city development from the beginning of this century to 1939; it is also, with the modification that the greater use of rapid transport and the higher national standard of living intensified the suburban exodus to the point of creating derelict central districts despite continued commercial expansion therein, the story of American city development. It is a story which obviously falsifies Howard's hopes. But it does not discredit his proposals. On the contrary, it is now becoming evident that if we had had the wisdom to follow those proposals, infinite injury to urban society might have been avoided.

History is not predetermined. Chance enters into events without doubt, but human will and human morality and intelligence no less. Admittedly there may be said to be an element of chance in the presence or absence of noble and resolute will on the part of adequate men in the right place at a critical time. But I cannot help thinking that if the inspiration and initiative of Howard, and the public spirit and planning genius of Unwin, had been reciprocated by courageous statesmanship on the part of one or two leaders in Whitehall or London County Hall between 1900 and 1929, this record would have been entirely different.

If Howard's ideas are now coming into their own, after forty years of neglect and unwise urban development, it is because individual men have absorbed them, passed them on, and related them to the changing scene. The Garden City Association took its part in the advocacy of public town planning, and when this administrative technique came to Britain with John Burns's Act of 1909, it was renamed the Garden Cities and Town Planning Association. In 1941, when planning technique had advanced to the stage of potentially controlling the national pattern of urban and rural lay-out, it became the Town and Country Planning Association. At one time, to Howard's personal distress, the Association was nearly swept into acceptance of the suburban flood as inevitable; but it has never been without a solid core of champions of the true Garden City principle. Among the leaders of the Association who upheld the essential idea when developmental fashion was against it, I mention (without disrespect to many others) the names of the late Herbert Warren, Mr. G. Montagu Harris, Mr. G. L. Pepler, Dr. Norman Macfadyen, Mr. C. B. Purdom, the Earl of Lytton, Lord Harmsworth, and Capt. R. L. Reiss. It was largely the persistence of the Association when the urban development of the inter-war years and the housing policy of the Government had intensified the nineteenth-century trend, that led to the appointment of the Barlow Royal Commission, and it was the evidence of the Association to that Commission that set the note of its Majority and Minority Reports. Serious national consideration of the principles first implied in Howard's book really only began with the publication of the Barlow Report in 1940 and the attention drawn to the possibility of the replanning of obsolete city areas by the German air-raids of 1940 and 1941.

Since then the evolution of public opinion on the subject has been prodigiously rapid. The Association founded by Howard seized the opportunity for public education in the larger issues. Economists, sociologists and public administrators woke up to the subject. And in 1944 the Government formally accepted the principles of decongestion of congested cities, of the dispersal of their 'overspill' of industry and population to new centres of life and work, and of the reservation of wide stretches of the countryside to form green belts separating towns—in short, the pattern of urban and rural development foreshadowed by Howard in his chapter on 'Social Cities'. At the time of writing, the Town and Country Planning Act 1944, the first piece of legislation definitely based on the principles of large-scale development under unified ownerships and of more open replanning and provision for relocation of displaced people and businesses in organic communities, has just been passed; and a nation-wide discussion is in progress as to the local application of those principles and as to the further legislation necessary to overcome the outstanding difficulties.[1]

[1] Since this Preface was written the Greater London Plan 1944 and the Regional Plan for Manchester have been published. The former

It is of interest to note that every one of the components of Howard's Garden City proposal has had in recent years its band of devotees, though many of them have ignored Howard and his movement and the devotees of the other components. Thus we have had in Britain a highly influential movement for the preservation of the agricultural countryside against ribbons of dwelling houses along main roads and scattered buildings in pleasant places. Another powerful movement specialized on the demand for playing fields and open spaces. Another attended to the need for local facilities for community life and popularized in Britain the theory, familiar for many years in America, of the 'neighbourhood unit'. Another concentrated on the aesthetic aspects of development, and agitated for architectural control of individual buildings and streets and groups of buildings. Others devoted themselves to better housing standards, tree planting, the control of advertisements, smoke abatement, rural rehabilitation, and the beautification of roads. The building of industrial 'trading estates' as a means of encouraging the settlement of factories in areas where industrial employment was desired, was undertaken by Government agencies. Each of these admirable causes has made a deep but separate impression on public opinion, and in the last few years their advocates have drawn closer together. Now that a synthesis is being attained, to what does it come? Precisely to the principles of development so lucidly expounded in this book, and exemplified in the two Garden Cities which Howard founded.

Let me now say a few words about Ebenezer Howard's life and personality. Born in 1850 at 62 Fore Street in the City of London, he was the son of a small shopkeeper and had no special advantages of class or education. At fifteen he became a clerk, drifting from one insignificant job to another till he was twenty-one, when he went to America with two friends, his intention to settle on the land there being due to the influence of a farmer uncle. He took up 160 acres of state

is the first fully worked-out plan for a metropolitan region embodying the Garden City principle. The Manchester Plan is notable for being based on a careful assessment of the amount of dispersal needed to bring down actual housing density to a proper standard.

18

land in Howard County, Nebraska, joined with his two associates in building a shanty, planted maize, potatoes, cucumbers and water-melons, and, not being temperamentally a farmer, was a dismal failure at the job. For a short time he hired himself to the one man of the three who proved able to make good on the land, but within a year he went to Chicago and resumed office employment. While a London clerk he had learned shorthand, and in Chicago, working for a firm of shorthand writers, he became an expert reporter for the courts and the press. Returning to England in 1876, he joined Gurneys, the official Parliamentary reporters, and after one unlucky attempt at a private partnership he settled down to working for Gurneys and other firms in the same business for the rest of his days. His life was always one of hard work and little income; his interest was never seriously in his own economic prosperity but was divided between mechanical invention and the movement which he created and which made him famous.

Once or twice between 1876 and 1898 he revisited America, in connection with his inventions and the introduction of the Remington typewriter to England. His inventions must I think have brought him less money than their development cost him, but they were a large part of his life, and almost always he had a small workshop somewhere in which a mechanic was working on his ideas. When obsessed with one of these ideas, he would persist with it in defiance of all advice from his friends as to its commercial prospects, and in this is one clue to his character.

In 1879 he married Elizabeth Ann Bills, daughter of a countryman-innkeeper of Nuneaton—a lady of distinguished personality, possessing high intelligence and taste and a deep love of the countryside. They had three daughters and a son, and nine grandchildren. Despite perpetual economic stringency the family life was a united and happy one. Mrs. Howard died in 1904, just when the building of Letchworth was beginning, but there is no doubt that her complementary interests and wise counsel were of much assistance to Howard in the development of his ideas and the writing of his book. In the short period between its publication and her death she was, by all reports, next to himself the most effective missionary for his proposals.

In his spare time the young Howard moved in earnest circles of Nonconformist churchmen and less orthodox religious enthusiasts, circles overlapping with others of mild reformists, who in those days were largely concerned with the land question. Henry George's Single Tax, Land Nationalization, and many other proposals relating land ownership and land values to the problems of poverty and urban squalor, were the mental food of such groups. No doubt Howard's movements between London and America, his experiences when reporting, and his business relationships, gave him a good background knowledge of affairs. His reading was not extensive, but he had a sharp eye for anything floating around that had relevance to his special interest.

Creative work always arises by the synthesis in one man's mind of material from otherwise unrelated sources, and it would be misleading to trace Howard's distinctive ideas to any single influence. If any one book may be said to have 'triggered off' the charge accumulating in Howard's mind, it was Bellamy's *Looking Backward*, the American edition of which aroused his enthusiasm in 1888 and which he was instrumental in having published in England. To a sceptical and sophisticated student of to-day that book seems a very mechanistic and politically immature Utopia, but it played a larger part than is commonly recognized in the inspiration of the rising British working-class movement. Its two basic assumptions—that technological advance could emancipate men from degrading toil, and that men are inherently co-operative and equalitarian—were the essence of Howard's own optimistic outlook, in which there was no proletarian resentment or class-bitterness, and not a trace of nostalgic anti-urbanism, anti-industrialism, or back-to-the-landism.

Let it be admitted that it is evidence of a certain innocence of political theory and inexperience in affairs that Howard should, in his own words, have 'swallowed whole' Bellamy's vision of the communistic Boston of A.D. 2000. He was in good company in this; more than one member of the British Cabinet may yet tell us in their memoirs that in their blissful youth they did the same. Howard proceeded to qualify the Bostonian's Utopia with great rapidity. Under the impact of the book the conception of an ideal town came to him as essentially a 'socialist community'. From the first it was to have a belt of rural land associated with it, every industry, including agriculture, being carried on collectively, as in Bellamy's dream, for the good of all. But at once Howard (perhaps remembering Nebraska) saw the difficulty of municipal agriculture, and this led to the thought: Why not leave agriculture to private enterprise on publicly owned land, so that any increments of value could be secured? He then extended this principle to the factories, shops and other businesses, and thus evolved, from an initially theoretical impulse, an entirely workable set-up. He did not derive the idea of the limitation of the size of the town, or of the permanent rural belt, from *Looking Backward*, because it is not expressed in that book—though Bellamy did come very near the same arrangement of town and country in his sequel *Equality*. Approximations to the Green-Belt principle can be traced back far into history, the most distinct formulation being in More's *Utopia*; but the route by which it reached Howard's mind is uncertain. It is beginning to stand out as one of the most important ingredients of the Garden City conception. But the conception as it finally emerged was Howard's own. It was, in his own words, 'a unique combination of proposals', including not only a clearer and more quantitative formulation of a desirable relationship between the industrial town and the agricultural background than any previous writer had produced, but also a well-worked-out machinery for a practical approach to the formulated pattern.

Howard—let me emphasize this—was not a political theorist, not a dreamer, but an inventor. The inventor proceeds by first conceiving an idea of a possible new product or instrument, next by evolving a design on paper with patient thought for the adaptation of the structure to the conditions it has to fulfil, and finally by experimentation with models to test the design in practice. Here in the text and diagrams of this book we have the paper-work of Howard's invention, and the completeness and judgment with which he worked out a problem involving extremely complex social and economic factors is none the less remarkable because he made his drawings and specification so simple. When it came to the experimental stage the designs had of course to be further developed and modified, but they proved to be fundamentally sound.

Of Howard's life story there is little more that I need tell. He went to live in his First Garden City in 1905, was a director of the estate company throughout, and took an active part in the public, social and religious life of the town. He transferred to his Second Garden City in 1921, and remained there till his death in 1928. As President of the International Housing and Town Planning Federation he became known and honoured all over the world. In 1927 he was knighted. He married again in 1907, and his second wife survived him till 1941.

Memorials to Ebenezer Howard exist in the form of a Children's Paddling Pool in Howard's Park, Letchworth, and a simple brick monument in Howardsgate (the central street named after him) at Welwyn Garden City. An annual Howard Memorial Lecture is delivered at Letchworth. The Howard Memorial Medal, for distinguished contributions to the development and advancement of the Garden City idea, has so far been awarded (by the Town and Country Planning Association) to the late Sir Raymond Unwin, F.R.I.B.A., Mr. Barry Parker, F.R.I.B.A., Professor Sir Patrick Abercrombie, F.R.I.B.A., Dr. Norman Macfadyen, M.B., and Professor Lewis Mumford (U.S.A.). At Letchworth the Mrs. Howard Memorial Hall was built in 1905 as a tribute to Ebenezer Howard's first wife.

Associations for the advocacy of Ebenezer Howard's Garden City proposals were established, at various dates from 1904 onwards, in France, Germany, Holland, Italy, Belgium, Poland, Czechoslovakia, Spain, Russia and the United States. Most of these have since been replaced by or merged in societies concerned with Town and Country Planning generally.

Howard's personality was a continual source of surprise to strangers knowing of his astonishing achievements. He was the mildest and most unassuming of men, unconcerned with his personal appearance, rarely giving evidence of the force within him. Of medium height and sturdy build, and always dressed in a rather shabbily conventional way, he was the sort of man who could easily pass unnoticed in a crowd; Mr. Bernard Shaw, who much admired what he did, only overstates a truth when he says that this 'amazing man' seemed an 'elderly nobody', 'whom the Stock Exchange would have dismissed as a negligible crank'. No discerning observer, however, could miss the signs of quality in his person. His most distinguished physical characteristics were a clear fresh complexion, a fine aquiline profile, and a really beautiful and powerful speaking voice, and it is not surprising that he was much in demand as an amateur Shakespearian actor in his younger days. He had a natural gift of eloquence; one of his early employers, the eminent Dr. Parker of the City Temple, was undoubtedly right in telling him that he could have been a successful preacher. He was universally liked, and notably by children.

On the platform and as a public figure he was most impressive and seemed of a dominating type; and yet in private and business life his associates tended to disregard him, even when carrying out the projects in which his initiative had involved them. Very largely this was due to his habitual mental preoccupation; he had little interest in administrative details, and full confidence that other men were well able to look after them; his inventor's mind, when at leisure from the grim grind of shorthand writing, was always revolving around some problem that he had set himself. His tremendous contribution to society was made possible by this concentration, by the fact that he seized upon a social problem of the first consequence, by the quiet daring of his intelligence, and, I would add, by his innate democratic sympathy and conviction of the value of human personality.

Howard's Garden City idea is coming into its own to-day, but not necessarily under his banner, and not without modifications. No one was better aware than he that inventions change as they develop. Whether the new communities of the future will be produced by the voluntary semi-co-operative machinery that Howard so ingeniously devised is a matter of interest, but not fundamental. The method may still prove a fruitful one among others, particularly if coupled, as Howard suggested, with the public acquisition of sites. In Great Britain the whole question of methods is being transformed by the evolution of statutory town and country planning and public guidance of the location of industry. Municipal ownership of town areas, with the organic planning of those areas by means of leasehold covenants, is already beginning to supplement public control of private development. It may be that the reservation of agricultural land by regional and local zoning will make it less necessary that green belts should be in the same ownership as the towns they encircle. And certainly a national system of Compensation and Betterment-collection would modify Howard's basis of Garden City finance.

Howard's synthesis has stood the test of experiment and the cross-examination of public controversy. It is I believe the key to the planning of the coming period. All its essential elements stand: moderate-sized industrial and trading towns in close contact with a surrounding agricultural countryside, each a healthy, well-equipped and coherent community; zoning of areas within each town for ready access between homes, workplaces, shops and cultural centres; limitation of density to safeguard light, gardens and recreation space, but not exaggerated to the pitch of urban diffusion; civic design aiming at harmony rather than standardization; planned internal and external communications; and unified site-ownership coupled with leaseholds, reconciling public interests with freedom of choice and enterprise.

Probably a modification of the first of these elements may be necessary in the case of the existing built-up areas of London and other huge agglomerations. In the inner areas of these cities Howard's country-belt may perforce be diminished to a parkstrip or the parkway 'perimeter-barrier' suggested in the Forshaw-Abercrombie Plan for London County. I have had my doubts of Howard's grand strategy of a flank attack on the congestion of the great cities: if we could, by rigorous agricultural zoning, stop their continuous outward spread, and by national standards of density in redevelopment, ensure their progressive opening-out, that procedure would appeal to me as less catastrophic and more humane. Recent planning thought in Great Britain, including the brilliant contribution of the Uthwatt Committee, has sought to find a means of recovering at least part of the heavy outlay involved in compensation for reducing the over-intensive use of land, by a levy on the increases of land value that will occur elsewhere. This line of approach, logical

24

and fair-minded as it is, may fail politically. Many people gravely question the financial practicability, and indeed the social justice, of payment by the State of full compensation for a degree of exploitation of land that is injurious to social welfare and never ought to have been allowed.

An intermediate course could theoretically be found by the 'time-limit' on uses of land no longer approved by public policy, and this was suggested by the Uthwatt Committee as part of a balanced solution of the whole problem. But it may be that a formula reasonably equating Compensation and Betterment, and acceptable to landowners as well as to the State, will not be found. It may be that the short-sightedness of some city authorities, and of some property interests, will in fact bring about the collapse in central values that Howard expected, without the compensation that his modern followers have proposed. A radical opening-out of congested cities, coupled with the building of new communities, must come, because the major social forces are now set in that direction, and the issues have become too clear for the history of the past half century to repeat itself. The new pattern of development does not necessarily entail the crisis that Howard foresaw for London and other great cities. They can forestall it by planned decongestion and dispersal to new towns, and a fair system of Compensation and Betterment-collection would greatly ease the transition if the parties can come to terms. It is by no means certain that Howard was wrong in his view that the creation of a number of new communities, and the movement of a considerable amount of industry (perhaps under State encouragement and guidance) away from the congested centres, will precede a solution of the land-value problem in those centres. But reservations on this and other points of detail and strategy in his book do not in the least weaken the force of his main argument.

Let it be remembered that in reading this book we are studying a blue-print nearly fifty years old. What is astonishing is not that it has faded on the edges, but that its centre remains so clear and bright.

PREFACE BY F. J. OSBORN

A Note on Terminology

Not only the term Garden City, but most of the terms used in discussion of the wider aspects of town and country planning, have been used in different senses, and the consequent confusion of discussion has affected policy. Gradually, as the elements of Garden City planning become the subjects of legislation and official orders, more standardization of terminology is likely to be achieved.

Garden City. Use of this term as a picturesque *sobriquet* of particular cities goes far back. Chicago (surprising as it seems at a distance) called itself The Garden City, through pride in its magnificent surroundings. Christchurch, founded in 1850, was known as the Garden City of New Zealand. The first place to be given Garden City as its official name appears to have been the New York suburb on Long Island started by Alexander T. Stewart in 1869. By 1900 there were, besides this one, nine villages and a small town in the United States named Garden City; how many there are now I do not know. Howard, who chose the term as meaning as much a city *in* a garden—that is surrounded by beautiful country—as a city *of* gardens, was unconscious of the Long Island use of the name when he adopted it. Its world-wide currency is due to his book; and the term as descriptive of a type of urban settlement should only be used in the sense which he gave to it. A short definition was adopted, in consultation with him, by the Garden Cities and Town Planning Association in 1919: 'A Garden City is a Town designed for healthy living and industry; of a size that makes possible a full measure of social life, but not larger; surrounded by a rural belt; the whole of the land being in public ownership or held in trust for the community.'

Garden Suburb, Garden Village. In these combinations the word Garden connotes simply a well-planned open lay-out. It is misleading, though good authorities have been guilty of the practice, to describe a Garden Suburb as a suburb 'laid out on Garden City lines'. The word Suburb is conveniently reserved for an outer part of a continuously built-up city, town, or urban area, implying that it is not separated therefrom by intervening country land. Thus a district so placed, and containing, besides dwellings, businesses serving only the local population, should be termed a Dormitory or Residential Suburb; and one so placed having industry as well, an Industrial Suburb. However well planned, such a place is wrongly called a Garden City or Satellite Town. The word Village implies small scale, detachment, and (I suggest) a basis which is primarily agricultural. Garden Village has been used as a name for a small settlement containing a factory and an associated openly planned housing estate; it should not however be used generically for such settlements if in a suburban situation.

Satellite Town. This term was first used in Great Britain in 1919 as an alternative description of Welwyn Garden City—a true Garden City in its scale, detachment, lay-out, structure, and basis of local employment. The reasons for adopting the new term were: first, the prevalent misuse of Garden City as synonymous with Open Suburb or Garden Suburb; second, recognition of a special economic linkage with Greater London. Some planning writers have thoughtlessly renewed the old confusion by using the term Satellite Town to describe a well-planned Industrial Suburb. It is better reserved for a Garden City or country town, at a moderate distance from a large city, but physically separated from that city by a Country Belt.

Country Belt, Agricultural Belt, Rural Belt. These terms are synonymous. They describe a stretch of countryside around and between towns, separating each from the others, and predominantly permanent farmland and parkland, whether or not such land is in the ownership of a town authority.

Green Belt. Originally used by Unwin as a further synonym for Country Belt, this term has also been applied, thus far confusingly, to a narrow strip of parkland more or less encircling part of a built-up metropolitan or large urban area. Park Belt is a better name for such a strip.

Decentralization, Dispersal, Diffusion. Till recently advocates of the Garden City idea have used Decentralization as the key-word for the planned movement of people and work-places from congested urban areas to detached smaller towns. In America it is often used to mean the spontaneous movement from the centre to the immediate outskirts of an urban area—quite a different thing. Lately the word Dispersal has been adopted for the former process; and this usage is now becoming standardized. As a planning term Dispersal does not connote a wide spreading of development over rural areas. For this latter process, if a technical label is needed, it is better to use the term Diffusion. Decentralization remains available as a general term for any outward movement. For the combined settlement of both industry and residents in suburbs I suggest the word Sub-Centralization.

Experience does not make me optimistic of a uniform use of planning terms. An attractive name, coming to be associated with an attractive form of development, rapidly acquires prestige. Men having sub-standard goods to offer will put the popular label thereon; and in time the odium attaching to the substitute will diminish the prestige of the label, and therefore of the original goods. That has happened to Garden City. It is now happening to Satellite Town, which has been applied to industrial excrescences on vast agglomerations, and to Green Belt, which has been applied to exiguous ribbons of park-space which you can almost step over without noticing. Perhaps we cannot prevent these perversions of good words by commercial and demagogic interests. But at least we should avoid them in planning literature.

Welwyn Garden City
September 1945

The Garden City Idea and Modern Planning
by Lewis Mumford

Garden Cities of To-morrow has done more than any other single book to guide the modern town planning movement and to alter its objectives. But it has met the traditional misfortune of the classic: it is denounced by those who have plainly never read it and it is sometimes accepted by those who have not fully understood it. Nothing could be a more timely contribution to building a life-centred civilization than the republication of Sir Ebenezer Howard's famous book.

At the beginning of the twentieth century two great new inventions took form before our eyes: the aeroplane and the Garden City, both harbingers of a new age: the first gave man wings and the second promised him a better dwelling-place when he came down to earth. Both inventions had originally been conceived by that brilliant, many-sided technician, Leonardo da Vinci; for he not merely studied the flight of birds to good purpose but proposed to abate the congestion and squalor of Milan by building a group of ten cities of five thousand houses, limited to thirty thousand inhabitants each, cities which, in another place, he proposed to design with a complete separation of pedestrian and horse traffic, and with gardens attached to a municipal irrigation system.

Ebenezer Howard was not influenced even at second hand by Leonardo, whose notebooks were not yet available in English; instead, he was in the tradition of a group of early nineteenth-century writers: Spence, the land reformer, who sought the nationalization of land; James Buckingham, who had published a plan for a model industrial town in 1848; Edward Gibbon Wakefield, who had pointed out the necessity for a more systematic plan of colonization for distant lands; and not least, two critical thinkers who were nearer at hand, Henry George and Peter Kropotkin. The work of these men gave substance to Howard's own intuitions and beliefs; but no little stimulus came to him from his visit to America, where he had before him the constant spectacle of new communities being laid out every year on new land, and he was impressed by the possibility of a fresh start.

Had Howard been a mere dreamer this book might have remained an object of curious discussion, like Edgard Chambless's *Roadtown*, which gave to the physical utilities of planning the priority that Howard, a far better sociologist, gave to social and economic arrangements. But Howard was a practical idealist, like the Rochdale co-operators before him; and he utilized the widespread interest in his idea to gather support for the planning and building of an experimental Garden City.

Howard's initiatives in the Garden City paralleled the Wright Brothers'. I emphasize this parallelism because it points to a functional relationship that has too often been overlooked even by those who have advocated the Garden City; for if the aeroplane, in its present or conceivable future forms, is to be anything but a menace to health and sanity and safety, and if it is to become as much a part of our daily life as the motor-car now is, it will be so only after the Garden City, with its wide belt of open land, has become the dominant urban form.

What were the leading ideas that have given Howard's theoretic exposition, and its first practical application in Letchworth Garden City, the immense influence that they have achieved? One would think, from a great many foolish allusions that one finds currently in both English and American discussions of town planning, that the sole characteristic of the Garden City was Howard's alleged plan for lowering the density of the population to twelve houses to the acre. Nothing could be more fantastic than this error: you will look in vain through the pages of *Garden Cities of To-morrow* for even the hint of such a proposal.

Furthermore, if by any chance Howard had framed such a notion, it should hardly have attracted attention; for there was nothing whatever new or startling in the mere suggestion that open planning is more salubrious than closed and congested planning. People had discovered that fact during the Middle Ages and had built their summer houses in the suburbs accordingly: in many early New England towns twelve houses to the acre would have seemed rather cramped; and the same fact would hold true of many English and American suburbs that have been built since the middle of the nineteenth century.

The preposterous notion that twelve houses per acre is specially identifiable with the Garden City could only have occurred to those who had not even a cursory knowledge of the actual development of cities during the last three hundred years. The whole subject of open planning versus closed planning is capable of rational discussion on its own grounds: but when some decision has been reached here, provisionally, it will be found that, whatever it is, it leaves the idea of the Garden City, as outlined by Ebenezer Howard, completely intact.

What actually happened was that during the very years that Howard was campaigning for the Garden City, Sir Raymond Unwin, the co-planner of Letchworth, demonstrated that even from an economic standpoint there is 'Nothing Gained by Overcrowding'. That demonstration was indeed a revolutionary one; and it had a powerful and well-deserved influence.

Unwin showed that vast amounts of money had been wasted in duplicating unnecessary streets and in robbing people of garden space, under the false notion that crowding houses together would reduce their costs: he thus documented the standard of twelve houses per acre which he had introduced into Letchworth and was later to apply in public housing when he was chief architect in the Ministry of Health. To attribute Unwin's discovery to Howard is to be fair to neither man.

Here let me say in passing, lest I be thought to avoid the issue of open versus closed planning, that Unwin's density of 36–48 per acre is closer to the standards I believe vital than the 136 per acre that the County of London Plan, for example, accepted. But I do not believe that 48 per acre is the highest number compatible with health and good living; and I would therefore criticize any rigid mechanical application of Unwin's standard. If I needed authority for this position I should find it in Howard's pages.

In the matter of density in housing, Ebenezer Howard's proposals were on the conservative side: in fact, they followed the traditional dimensions that had been handed down since the Middle Ages, and, one may add by way of criticism, followed

31

them too closely. For Howard specifically said that the average size of a building lot was 20 by 130, while the minimum was 20 by 100. This twenty-foot front is far too narrow for a good modern building row, with relatively shallow rooms, fully open to the penetration of the sun's rays. But the densities so provided are those of the traditional city before overbuilding took place: 20 by 100 is, for example, the typical New York City lot. With five people to a family this gave a density (allowing for cross-roads) of about 90 to 95 persons per residential acre, and with our smaller family units would give a density of about 70 per acre.

Indeed, in the concrete details of planning Howard was still under the spell of the age that lay behind him. His Crystal Palace Road, with its great shopping district under glass, facing a wide open space, partly reminds one of Princes Street in Edinburgh; but even more it recalls the glass-covered streets of that early Victorian Buckingham, if not the fantasies of Mr. H. G. Wells. Howard did indeed make one brilliant technical innovation which has passed almost unnoticed and was forgotten in the development of the garden cities that followed: this was in his conception of the Grand Avenue, 'a belt of green, upwards of three miles long', dividing the town into two separate zones. Such an internal green belt, for separating the functional elements of the city, suggests a pattern that has still fully to be realized: one sketched out in the report on Honolulu (*Whither Honolulu?*) which the writer submitted to the City and County Park Board in 1938.

Howard's greatness did not lie in the field of technical planning, and no one knew this better than he did: every concrete sketch of the new type of city is carefully labelled with a warning that what he has set down is only a diagram, and that the actual city would have to be an adaptation of this diagram to actual conditions. When Messrs. Unwin and Parker came to design Letchworth itself, they perhaps leaned over backwards, in their effort to avoid mechanical stereotypes, in order not to duplicate Howard's diagrammatic city. Unwin's love for the rambling layout of medieval German hill towns was even in some degree at war with Howard's rational clarifications and forward-looking proposals.

But the important point to remember is that the Garden City principle deals with the constants in planning: the idea itself does not stand or fall with the successes or mistakes of Letchworth or Welwyn; neither can Howard's contribution be lightly set aside by those who have, at a later date, been led to make a similar analysis and have possessively given the central idea a new name. Plainly, like every other invention, Howard's Garden City is open to successive improvements in detail: moreover, the idea would give rise to one type of city in Hertfordshire or Buckinghamshire and another in the San Bernardino Valley in California or in the Columbia River Valley of the Northwest. It is precisely because Howard was in practice both a sociologist and a statesman that his proposals have this universal quality.

Howard's prime contribution was to outline the nature of a balanced community and to show what steps were necessary, in an ill-organized and disoriented society, to bring it into existence. On one side was the overgrown and over-congested metropolis penalized in its health by its slums, and in its efficiency by ill-sorted and misplaced industries, given to extravagant wastes in time and energy and money merely to transport its goods and people over distances that had been expanded for no good human purpose, desolate in its lack of social facilities, though possessing, in its central institutions, the chief organized forms of social life. The continued growth of centres like London, Paris, and Berlin, and their imitators lower down in the urban scale, had not resulted in any commensurate gains in social life. Hence the increase of population and wealth in our big centres had paradoxically resulted in destitution, and no small part of the city's income was concerned with alleviating this destitution by costly measures of sanitation and slum clearance.

The country, on the other hand, was equally impoverished: emptied out of its more able and enterprising spirits by the very growth of big cities. Here were fresh air, sunlight, pleasant vistas, quiet nights, all scarce commodities in the big cities; but on the other hand, there was another sort of destitution, a dearth of human companionship and of co-operative effort. Agriculture, having lost much of its local market, was a declining occupation, and life in a country town was as mean, illiberal, and dismal as life in a metropolitan slum. Nor would decentralization of single industries into the open country help matters here: for if man is to live a balanced life, capable of calling out all his faculties and bringing them to perfection, he must live in a community that fully sustains them. What was needed, Howard saw—as Kropotkin at the same time proclaimed—was a marriage of town and country, of rustic health and sanity and activity and urban knowledge, urban technical facility, urban political co-operation. The instrument of that marriage was the Garden City.

Here again I must utter a warning against those who mistake Howard's programme for one of breaking down the distinction of town and country and turning them into an amorphous suburban mass. The reader who has the patience to follow Howard's argument will see that he had no such end in mind; indeed, the whole project is an attempt to guard against its happening.

For the Garden City, as conceived by Howard, is not a loose indefinite sprawl of individual houses with immense open spaces over the whole landscape: it is rather a compact, rigorously confined urban grouping. Of the total tract to be included in the domain of the Garden City, one thousand acres, at the centre, were to be occupied by the city itself; and five thousand acres formed an agricultural green belt. Thirty thousand people were to live on those thousand acres; 30 per gross acre as compared with 57 per gross acre in the present congested, park-destitute county of London. Parks were provided within the Garden City on the basis of a little more than nine acres per thousand; well above the four acres suggested in the new plan for London, but not so much higher than the six that Westminster normally boasts. It may be argued that Howard's town-density is greater than would be generally acceptable; he cannot be accused of being an advocate of urban sprawl.

Where then did Howard's originality lie? Not in special details, but in his characteristic synthesis; in particular these proposals: the provision of a permanent belt of open land, to be used for agriculture as an integral part of the city; the use of this land to limit the physical spread of the city from within, or encroachments from urban development not under control at the perimeter; the permanent ownership and control of the entire urban tract by the municipality itself and its disposition by means of leases into private hands; the limitation of population to the number originally planned for the area; the reservation for the community of the unearned increment from the growth and prosperity of the city, up to the limits of growth fixed; the moving into the new urban area of industries capable of supporting the greater part of its population; the provision for founding new communities as soon as the existing land and social facilities are occupied.

In short, Howard attacked the whole problem of the city's development, not merely its physical growth but the interrelationship of urban functions within the community and the integration of urban and rural patterns, for the vitalizing of urban life on one hand and the intellectual and social improvement of rural life on the other.

In treating rural and urban improvement as a single problem, Howard was far in advance of his age; and he was a better diagnostician of urban decay than many of our own contemporaries. His Garden City was not only an attempt to relieve the congestion of the big city, and by so doing lower the land values and prepare the way for metropolitan reconstruction: it was equally an attempt to do away with that inevitable correlate of metropolitan congestion, the suburban dormitory, whose open plan and nearer access to the country are only temporary, and whose lack of an industrial population and a working base make it one of the most unreal environments ever created for man: a preposterous middle-class counterpart to the courtly inanities of those absolute monarchs who, at Versailles or Nymphenburg, contrived for themselves a disconnected playworld of their own. *The Garden City, as Howard defined it, is not a suburb but the antithesis of a suburb: not a more rural retreat, but a more integrated foundation for an effective urban life.*

Howard saw that there was no solution of the city's problems within the existing framework of municipal administration, because one of its greatest problems was the lack of economic and social and political relation to the surrounding countryside:

here his vision was far clearer than the vision of those municipal reformers and those housing experts who have let themselves become absorbed in some single aspect of urban development and have forgotten the larger situation of which the narrow problem they have chosen to solve is but a part. What Howard said about the relation of town and country within the Garden City area is equally applicable to the entire business of city and regional planning: the administrative unit that is created must be capable of embracing both the urban and the rural aspects of the region.

Not the least part of Howard's conception was his emphasis upon the *grouping* of Garden Cities: he realized that the advantages of a single city would be multiplied by the creation of 'town-clusters', groups or constellations of such cities. But with his resolute sense of the practical, he first proposed to make an experimental demonstration with a single Garden City. Unlike many bold dreamers, he not merely helped to bring Letchworth into existence; but in time he founded a second city, Welwyn. Meanwhile the ideas Howard had expounded were to become the common property of planners all over the world and were to influence the planning of Hilversum in the Netherlands, Ernst May's satellite communities in Frankfort-am-Main, and Wright and Stein's Radburn.

Here we must touch on Howard's qualifications as a statesman; for he was a statesman in the sense that J. W. Mitchell of the co-operative movement was a statesman; and his life work demonstrates the best qualities of British statecraft, for with all Howard's sense of the moment and the passing opportunity, he was not, like too many of our contemporaries, afraid of rational plans and long-term commitments. Howard's mind was the English mind at its best: always in touch with the practicable, always in sight of the ideal. He believed consistently in the experimental method; and he felt that in political life, no less than in science, a crucial experiment would carry such conviction that those who had been opposed to the abstract scheme would be convinced no less than those who had favoured it. 'Would it not . . . be better to study a smaller problem first, and to paraphrase [Nunquam's] words, "Given, say, 6,000 acres of land, let us endeavour to make the best use of it"'? For then, having dealt with this, we shall have educated ourselves to deal with a larger area.' This is the way that rational men should think and act. With his gift of sweet reasonableness Howard hoped to win Tory and Anarchist, single-taxer and socialist, individualist and collectivist, over to his experiment. And his hopes were not altogether discomfited; for in appealing to the English instinct for finding common ground he was utilizing a solid political tradition.

At this distance, what strikes one about Howard's Garden City proposals was how little he was concerned with the outward form of the new city and how much he was concerned with the processes that would produce such communities. He did not win support by publishing meretricious pictures of the City Beautiful or by pretending life would be changed out of recognition in this new environment. He pleaded for definite improvements along lines that had already been accepted: he trusted to change by 'the force of example, that is, by setting up a better system and by a little skill in the grouping of forces and the manipulation of ideas.' In this grouping and manipulation lay his strength as a thinker. And in one of the concluding chapters, called Social Cities, he looked forward to the step beyond experimental demonstration. 'Railways', he observed, 'were first made without statutory powers. They were constructed on a very small scale. . . . But when the "Rocket" was built and the supremacy of the locomotive fully established, it then became necessary, if railway enterprise was to go forward, to obtain legislative powers.'

Sir Ebenezer did not take the second step he had originally envisaged so clearly: with the impatience of an old man, he sought to duplicate his original success instead of widening it out into broader channels. At the end of the last war, his younger lieutenant, Mr. F. J. Osborn, proposed to build 'New Towns after the War', on a scale commensurate with the current needs for housing and rehousing: a proposal that required complete legislative backing. Howard's absorption in the launching of the second garden city diverted energy from the more important work that Mr. Osborn had outlined; and the broad political need to unite housing and industrial rehabilitation with urban improvement was subordinated to a muddled and wasteful effort at town extension and estate building within the existing municipal areas.

Only during the last decade has our thinking on the subject of housing and community planning become political. The Barlow Report in Great Britain has taken up the process of urban improvement at the point where Howard in his old age abandoned it. Now the great need of the moment is to harness the entire process of urban building to the substantial innovations in municipal economics and planning that Sir Ebenezer Howard originally set forth.

By now, our neotechnic and biotechnic facilities have at last caught up with Howard's and Kropotkin's intuitions. Howard's plan for canalizing the flow of population, diverting it from the existing centres to new centres; his plan for decentralizing industry and setting up both city and industry within a rural matrix, the whole planned to a human scale, is technologically far more feasible to-day than it was forty or fifty years ago. For in the meanwhile, our new means of instantaneous communication have multiplied; likewise our means for swift transport; and points that are fifty miles apart are now as close, provided the Garden City pattern of development is followed, as points five miles apart were in the congested metropolis of yesterday.

Meanwhile, the need for balanced communities has deepened; for the task of our age is to work out an urban environment that will be just as favourable to fertility, just as encouraging to marriage and parenthood, as rural areas still are. Howard, at the time he first wrote, had no reason to be concerned with the threat of a declining population; but it happens —so organic, so deeply biotechnic, was his whole conception— that the sort of city he projected was precisely the kind whose population will be biologically capable of reproducing itself and psychologically disposed to do so. With the prospects of a dwindling population if the past tendencies toward urban concentration continue, the question now becomes not whether Britain and the United States can afford to build Garden Cities, but whether they can afford to build anything else.

So far I have dealt with Howard's thought in relation to its immediate environment. But the ideas for which he stood have no national boundaries; and the kind of urban organization he favoured has an importance for the United States for the same basic reasons that it has for England. Our own tradition of city building includes the New England village which was indeed originally an informal kind of Garden City; it includes the early New England factory town, which, as Mr. John Coolidge has shown, embodied some very admirable efforts in both town planning and housing; and not least it includes a multitude of utopian centres from the Shaker communities in New York and Massachusetts to Salt Lake City in Utah in which an effort was made to establish higher physical and social standards. Meanwhile, the over-canny and socially disruptive speculation which produced the great mass of our industrial and commercial centres has created vast areas of blight that cry as loudly for reorganization and rebuilding as the bombed areas of Britain.

Here, too, partial experimental efforts have been made in the right direction, from the communities erected by the U.S. Shipping Board in 1918 to the Greenbelt Towns that were created by the Resettlement Administration in 1936—not least Greenbelt, Maryland, itself. But, as in England, reformers and politicians have avoided an integral attack upon the problem of civic and rural reconstruction and have confined themselves to the demolition of slums and to the building of a multitude of housing communities, some of which are, by their very constitution, the slums of to-morrow, if not already the slums of to-day. Nowhere is there a greater need for the kind of fundamental thinking that Howard applied to city building than in the United States; and nowhere is there greater need for proceeding from experimental action to broad legislative powers.

Nor is it only in the older portions of the United States that decentralization by Garden Cities is needed: Howard's broad programme should find its boldest applications in the more recently settled sections of the United States, particularly in California and the Pacific Northwest, where the tendency to funnel the population into vast amorphous urban areas like Los Angeles, the San Francisco Bay Region, Portland, and Seattle will not merely delay the many-sided exploitation of the natural resources of this area, but will undermine a native birthrate already sagging as badly as that of Sweden or Great Britain.

The most important thinking that has been done in the United

States during the last decade on the elements of planning has, probably, been the work of the National Resources Planning Board and its state affiliates: yet nothing shows how defective our preparation for such work has been so much as the fact that the problem of regional development has been separated from that of city development; so that the report on *Our Cities* deals almost exclusively with cities as self-sustaining entities, and particularly with metropolitan areas, while the reports on resources and industrial opportunities stop short at the outskirts of the city. There is hardly a portion of this work that would not have been more significant and more effective had the investigators and planners fully absorbed the great lessons first expounded in Howard's *Garden Cities of To-morrow*.

Happily it is not too late to make good this deficiency. Before too many billions of dollars are sunk in cramped misplaced housing, misconceived road systems funnelling into metropolitan areas, extravagantly extended suburbs, and misplanned slum clearances and rebuildings, it would be well for those who have not read Howard's book, or have not grappled with it, to go carefully over his thesis and to absorb all its implications. This is not merely a book for technicians: above all it is a book for citizens, for the people whose actively expressed needs, desires, and interests should guide the planner and administrator at every turn. Letchworth and Welwyn themselves have still something to teach the American planner, but *Garden Cities of To-morrow*, the repository of the ideas that begot Letchworth and Welwyn, has still far more to teach. Howard's ideas have laid the foundation for a new cycle in urban civilization: one in which the means of life will be subservient to the purposes of living, and in which the pattern needed for biological survival and economic efficiency will likewise lead to social and personal fulfilment.

Amenia, New York
   September 1945

Author's Introduction

'New forces, new cravings, new aims, which had been silently gathering beneath the crust of reaction, burst suddenly into view.'—
J. R. GREEN, *Short History of the English People*, Chap. x.

'Change is consummated in many cases after much argument and agitation, and men do not observe that almost everything has been silently effected by causes to which few people paid any heed. In one generation an institution is unassailable, in the next bold men may assail it, and in the third bold men defend it. At one time the most conclusive arguments are advanced against it in vain, if indeed they are allowed utterance at all. At another time the most childish sophistry is enough to secure its condemnation. In the first place, the institution, though probably indefensible by pure reason, was congruous with the conscious habits and modes of thought of the community. In the second, these had changed from influences which the acutest analysis would probably fail to explain, and a breath sufficed to topple over the sapped structure.'—*The Times*, 27th November 1891.

In these days of strong party feeling and of keenly contested social and religious issues, it might perhaps be thought difficult to find a single question having a vital bearing upon national life and well-being on which all persons, no matter of what political party, or of what shade of sociological opinion, would be found to be fully and entirely agreed. Discuss the temperance cause, and you will hear from Mr. John Morley that it is 'the greatest moral movement since the movement for the abolition of slavery'; but Lord Bruce will remind you that 'every year the trade contributes £40,000,000 to the revenue of the country, so that practically it maintains the Army and Navy, besides which it affords employment to many thousands of persons'—that 'even the teetotallers owe much to the licensed victuallers, for if it were not for them the refreshment bars at the Crystal Palace would have been closed long ago'. Discuss the opium traffic, and, on the one hand, you will hear that opium is rapidly destroying the *morale* of the people of China, and, on the other, that this is quite a delusion, and that the Chinese are capable, thanks to opium, of doing work which to a European is quite impossible, and that on food at which the least squeamish of English people would turn up their noses in disgust.

Religious and political questions too often divide us into hostile camps; and so, in the very realms where calm, dispassionate thought and pure emotions are the essentials of all advance towards right beliefs and sound principles of action, the din of battle and the struggles of contending hosts are more forcibly suggested to the onlooker than the really sincere love of truth and love of country which, one may yet be sure, animate nearly all breasts.

There is, however, a question in regard to which one can scarcely find any difference of opinion. It is wellnigh universally agreed by men of all parties, not only in England, but all over Europe and America and our colonies, that it is deeply to be deplored that the people should continue to stream into the already over-crowded cities, and should thus further deplete the country districts.

Lord Rosebery, speaking some years ago as Chairman of the London County Council, dwelt with very special emphasis on this point:

'There is no thought of pride associated in my mind with the idea of London. I am always haunted by the awfulness of London: by the great appalling fact of these millions cast down, as it would appear by hazard, on the banks of this noble stream, working each in their own groove and their own cell, without regard or knowledge of each other, without heeding each other, without having the slightest idea how the other lives—the heedless casualty of unnumbered thousands of men. Sixty years ago a great Englishman, Cobbett, called it a wen. If it was a wen then, what is it now? A tumour, an elephantiasis sucking into its gorged system half the life and the blood and the bone of the rural districts.' (March 1891.)

Sir John Gorst points out the evil, and suggests the remedy:

'If they wanted a permanent remedy of the evil they must remove the cause; they must back the tide, and stop the migration of the people into the towns, and get the people back to the land. The interest and the safety of the towns themselves were

42

involved in the solution of the problem.' (*Daily Chronicle*, 6th November 1891.)

Dean Farrar says:

'We are becoming a land of great cities. Villages are stationary or receding; cities are enormously increasing. And if it be true that great cities tend more and more to become the graves of the physique of our race, can we wonder at it when we see the houses so foul, so squalid, so ill-drained, so vitiated by neglect and dirt?'

Dr. Rhodes, at the Demographic Congress, called attention to 'the migration which was going on from the English agricultural districts. In Lancashire and other manufacturing districts 35 per cent of the population were over sixty years of age, but in agricultural districts they would have over 60 per cent.[1] Many of the cottages were so abominable that they could not call them houses, and the people so deteriorated in physique that they were not able to do the amount of work which able-bodied persons should do. Unless something was done to make the lot of the agricultural labourer better, the exodus would go on, with what results in the future he dared not say.' (*Times*, 15th August 1891.)

The Press, Liberal, Radical, and Conservative, views this grave symptom of the time with the same alarm. The *St. James's Gazette*, on 6th June 1892, remarks:

'How best to provide the proper antidote against the greatest danger of modern existence is a question of no mean significance.'

The Star, 9th October 1891, says:

'How to stem the drift from the country is one of the main problems of the day. The labourer may perhaps be restored to the land, but how will the country industries be restored to rural England?'

The Daily News, a few years ago, published a series of articles, 'Life in our Villages', dealing with the same problem.

---

[1] This quotation is left as it originally appeared, but there must be a mistake in placing the decimal point. In 1939, the persons over 65 were, in the urban areas of England and Wales 8·77 per cent of the population, in Greater London 8·33 per cent, and in the rural districts 10·3 per cent. *Ed.*

Trade Unionist leaders utter the same note of warning. Mr. Ben Tillett says:

'Hands are hungry for toil, and lands are starving for labour.'

Mr. Tom Mann observes:

'The congestion of labour in the metropolis is caused mainly by the influx from the country districts of those who were needed there to cultivate the land.'

All, then, are agreed on the pressing nature of this problem, all are bent on its solution, and though it would doubtless be quite Utopian to expect a similar agreement as to the value of any remedy that may be proposed, it is at least of immense importance that, on a subject thus universally regarded as of supreme importance, we have such a consensus of opinion at the outset. This will be the more remarkable and the more hopeful sign When it is shown, as I believe will be conclusively shown in this work, that the answer to this, one of the most pressing questions of the day, makes of comparatively easy solution many other problems which have hitherto taxed the ingenuity of the greatest thinkers and reformers of our time. Yes, the key to the problem how to restore the people to the land—that beautiful land of ours, with its canopy of sky, the air that blows upon it, the sun that warms it, the rain and dew that moisten it —the very embodiment of Divine love for man—is indeed a *Master Key*, for it is the key to a portal through which, even when scarce ajar, will be seen to pour a flood of light on the problems of intemperance, of excessive toil, of restless anxiety, of grinding poverty—the true limits of Governmental interference, ay, and even the relations of man to the Supreme Power.

It may perhaps be thought that the first step to be taken towards the solution of this question—how to restore the people to the land—would involve a careful consideration of the very numerous causes which have hitherto led to their aggregation in large cities. Were this the case, a very prolonged enquiry would be necessary at the outset. Fortunately, alike for writer and for reader, such an analysis is not, however, here requisite, and for a very simple reason, which may be stated thus: Whatever may have been the causes which have operated in the past, and are operating now, to draw the people into the cities, those causes may all be summed up as 'attractions'; and it is obvious, therefore, that no remedy can possibly be effective which will not present to the people, or at least to considerable portions of them, greater 'attractions' than our cities now possess, so that the force of the old 'attractions' shall be overcome by the force of new 'attractions' which are to be created. Each city may be regarded as a magnet, each person as a needle; and, so viewed, it is at once seen that nothing short of the discovery of a method for constructing magnets of yet greater power than our cities possess can be effective for redistributing the population in a spontaneous and healthy manner.

So presented, the problem may appear at first sight to be difficult, if not impossible, of solution. 'What', some may be disposed to ask, 'can possibly be done to make the country more attractive to a workaday people than the town—to make wages, or at least the standard of physical comfort, higher in the country than in the town; to secure in the country equal possibilities of social intercourse, and to make the prospects of advancement for the average man or woman equal, not to say superior, to those enjoyed in our large cities?' The issue one constantly finds presented in a form very similar to that. The subject is treated continually in the public press, and in all forms of discussion, as though men, or at least working men, had not now, and never could have, any choice or alternative, but either, on the one hand, to stifle their love for human society—at least in wider relations than can be found in a straggling village—or, on the other hand, to forgo almost entirely all the keen and pure delights of the country. The question is universally considered as though it were now, and for ever must remain, quite impossible for working people to live in the country and yet be engaged in pursuits other than agricultural; as though crowded, unhealthy cities were the last word of economic science; and as if our present form of industry, in which sharp lines divide agricultural from industrial pursuits, were necessarily an enduring one. This fallacy is the very common one of ignoring altogether the possibility of alternatives other than those presented to the mind. There are in reality not only, as is so constantly assumed, two alternatives—town life and country life—but a third alternative, in which all the advantages of the most energetic and active town life, with all the beauty and delight of the country,

45

may be secured in perfect combination; and the certainty of being able to live this life will be the magnet which will produce the effect for which we are all striving—the spontaneous movement of the people from our crowded cities to the bosom of our

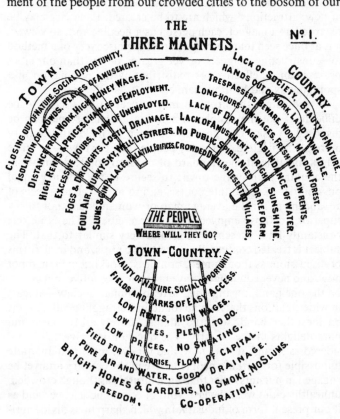

THE THREE MAGNETS

kindly mother earth, at once the source of life, of happiness, of wealth, and of power. The town and the country may, therefore, be regarded as two magnets, each striving to draw the people to itself—a rivalry which a new form of life, partaking of the nature of both, comes to take part in. This may be illustrated

46

by a diagram of 'The Three Magnets', in which the chief advantages of the Town and of the Country are set forth with their corresponding drawbacks, while the advantages of the Town-Country are seen to be free from the disadvantages of either.

The Town magnet, it will be seen, offers, as compared with the Country magnet, the advantages of high wages, opportunities for employment, tempting prospects of advancement, but these are largely counterbalanced by high rents and prices. Its social opportunities and its places of amusement are very alluring, but excessive hours of toil, distance from work, and the 'isolation of crowds' tend greatly to reduce the value of these good things. The well-lit streets are a great attraction, especially in winter, but the sunlight is being more and more shut out, while the air is so vitiated that the fine public buildings, like the sparrows, rapidly become covered with soot, and the very statues are in despair. Palatial edifices and fearful slums are the strange, complementary features of modern cities.

The Country magnet declares herself to be the source of all beauty and wealth; but the Town magnet mockingly reminds her that she is very dull for lack of society, and very sparing of her gifts for lack of capital. There are in the country beautiful vistas, lordly parks, violet-scented woods, fresh air, sounds of rippling water; but too often one sees those threatening words, 'Trespassers will be prosecuted'. Rents, if estimated by the acre, are certainly low, but such low rents are the natural fruit of low wages rather than a cause of substantial comfort; while long hours and lack of amusements forbid the bright sunshine and the pure air to gladden the hearts of the people. The one industry, agriculture, suffers frequently from excessive rainfalls; but this wondrous harvest of the clouds is seldom properly ingathered, so that, in times of drought, there is frequently, even for drinking purposes, a most insufficient supply.[1] Even the

[1] Dr. Barwise, Medical Officer of Health for the County Council of Derbyshire, giving evidence before a Select Committee of the House of Commons, on 25th April 1894, on the Chesterfield Gas and Water Bill, said, in answer to Question 1873: 'At Brimington Common School I saw some basins full of soapsuds, and it was all the water that the whole of the children had to wash in. They had to wash one after another in the same water. Of course, a child with

natural healthfulness of the country is largely lost for lack of proper drainage and other sanitary conditions, while, in parts almost deserted by the people, the few who remain are yet frequently huddled together as if in rivalry with the slums of our cities.

But neither the Town magnet nor the Country magnet represents the full plan and purpose of nature. Human society and the beauty of nature are meant to be enjoyed together. The two magnets must be made one. As man and woman by their varied gifts and faculties supplement each other, so should town and country. The town is the symbol of society—of mutual help and friendly co-operation, of fatherhood, motherhood, brotherhood, sisterhood, of wide relations between man and man—of broad, expanding sympathies—of science, art, culture, religion. And the country! The country is the symbol of God's love and care for man. All that we are and all that we have comes from it. Our bodies are formed of it; to it they return. We are fed by it, clothed by it, and by it are we warmed and sheltered. On its bosom we rest. Its beauty is the inspiration of art, of music, of poetry. Its forces propel all the wheels of industry. It is the source of all health, all wealth, all knowledge. But its fullness of joy and wisdom has not revealed itself to man. Nor can it ever, so long as this unholy, unnatural separation of society and nature endures. Town and country *must be married*, and out of this joyous union will spring a new hope, a new life, a new civilization. It is the purpose of this work to show how a first step can be taken in this direction by the construction of a Town-country magnet; and I hope to convince the reader that this is practicable, here and now, and that on principles which are the very soundest, whether viewed from the ethical or the economic standpoint.

I will undertake, then, to show how in 'Town-country' equal, nay better, opportunities of social intercourse may be enjoyed than are enjoyed in any crowded city, while yet the beauties of

ringworm or something of that kind might spread it through the whole of the children. . . . The schoolmistress told me that the children came in from the playground hot, and she had seen them actually drink this dirty water. In fact, when they were thirsty there was no other water for them to have.'

nature may encompass and enfold each dweller therein; how higher wages are compatible with reduced rents and rates; how abundant opportunities for employment and bright prospects of advancement may be secured for all; how capital may be attracted and wealth created; how the most admirable sanitary conditions may be ensured; how beautiful homes and gardens may be seen on every hand; how the bounds of freedom may be widened, and yet all the best results of concert and co-operation gathered in by a happy people.

The construction of such a magnet, could it be effected, followed, as it would be, by the construction of many more, would certainly afford a solution of the burning question set before us by Sir John Gorst, 'how to back the tide of migration of the people into the towns, and to get them back upon the land'.

A fuller description of such a magnet and its mode of construction will form the theme of subsequent chapters.

Chapter One

The Town-Country Magnet

'I will not cease from mental strife,
  Nor shall my sword sleep in my hand,
Till we have built Jerusalem
  In England's green and pleasant land.'
—BLAKE.

'Thorough sanitary and remedial action in the houses that we have; and then the building of more, strongly, beautifully, and in groups of limited extent, kept in proportion to their streams and walled round, so that there may be no festering and wretched suburb anywhere, but clean and busy street within and the open country without, with a belt of beautiful garden and orchard round the walls, so that from any part of the city perfectly fresh air and grass and sight of far horizon might be reachable in a few minutes' walk. This final aim.'—JOHN RUSKIN, *Sesame and Lilies.*

The reader is asked to imagine an estate embracing an area of 6,000 acres, which is at present purely agricultural, and has been obtained by purchase in the open market at a cost of £40[1] an acre, or £240,000. The purchase money is supposed to have been raised on mortgage debentures, bearing interest at an average rate not exceeding £4 per cent.[2] The estate is legally vested in the names of four gentlemen of responsible position and of undoubted probity and honour, who hold it in trust, first, as a security for the debenture-holders, and, secondly, in

[1] This was the average price paid for agricultural land in 1898; and, though this estimate may prove far more than sufficient, it is hardly likely to be much exceeded.

[2] The financial arrangements described in this book are likely to be departed from in form, but not in essential principle. And until a definite scheme has been agreed upon, I think it better to repeat them precisely as they appeared in *To-morrow*, the original title of this book—the book which led to the formation of the Garden City Association. (Footnote to 1902 edition. *Ed.*)

trust for the people of Garden City, the Town-country magnet, which it is intended to build thereon. One essential feature of the plan is that all ground rents, which are to be based upon the annual value of the land, shall be paid to the trustees, who, after providing for interest and sinking fund, will hand the balance to the Central Council of the new municipality,[1] to be employed by such Council in the creation and maintenance of all necessary public works—roads, schools, parks, etc.

The objects of this land purchase may be stated in various ways, but it is sufficient here to say that some of the chief objects are these: To find for our industrial population work at wages of *higher purchasing power*, and to secure healthier surroundings and more regular employment. To enterprising manufacturers, co-operative societies, architects, engineers, builders, and mechanicians of all kinds, as well as to many engaged in various professions, it is intended to offer a means of securing new and better employment for their capital and talents, while to the agriculturists at present on the estate as well as to those who may migrate thither, it is designed to open a new market for their produce close to their doors. Its object is, in short, to raise the standard of health and comfort of all true workers of whatever grade—the means by which these objects are to be achieved being a healthy, natural, and economic combination of town and country life, and this on land owned by the municipality.

Garden City, which is to be built near the centre of the 6,000 acres, covers an area of 1,000 acres, or a sixth part of the 6,000 acres, and might be of circular form, 1,240 yards (or nearly three-quarters of a mile) from centre to circumference. (Diagram 2 is a ground plan of the whole municipal area, showing the town in the centre; and Diagram 3, which represents one section or ward of the town, will be useful in following the description of the town itself—*a description which is, however, merely suggestive, and will probably be much departed from.*)

Six magnificent boulevards—each 120 feet wide—traverse the city from centre to circumference, dividing it into six equal parts or wards. In the centre is a circular space containing about

---

[1] This word, 'municipality', is not used in a technical sense.

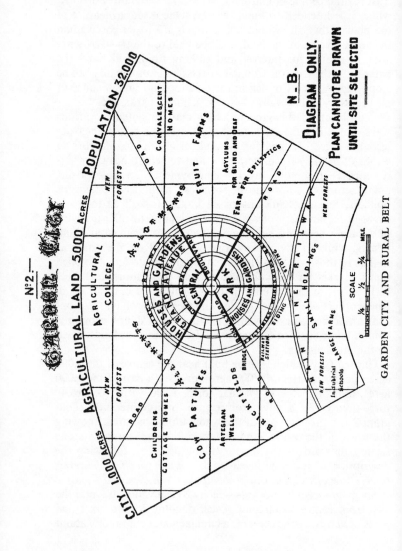

— No. 2 —
GARDEN-CITY

POPULATION 32,000

AGRICULTURAL LAND 5,000 ACRES

CITY 1,000 ACRES

N.B.
DIAGRAM ONLY.
PLAN CANNOT BE DRAWN
UNTIL SITE SELECTED

CONVALESCENT HOMES

NEW FORESTS

ROAD

ALLOTMENTS

FRUIT FARMS

AGRICULTURAL COLLEGE

ASYLUMS FOR BLIND AND DEAF

FARM FOR EPILEPTICS

ROAD

NEW FORESTS

MAIN LINE RAILWAY

SMALL HOLDINGS

SIDING

HOUSES AND GARDENS

CENTRAL PARK

GRAND AVENUE

RAILWAY STATION

BRIDGE

ALLOTMENTS

CHILDRENS COTTAGE HOMES

NEW FORESTS

ROAD

COW PASTURES

ARTESIAN WELLS

BRICKFIELDS

NEW FORESTS

INDUSTRIAL SCHOOLS

LARGE FARMS

SCALE
0   ¼   ½   ¾   MILE

GARDEN CITY AND RURAL BELT

52

five and a half acres, laid out as a beautiful and well-watered garden; and, surrounding this garden, each standing in its own ample grounds, are the larger public buildings—town hall,

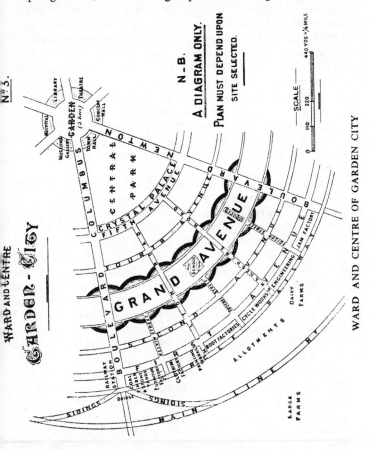

principal concert and lecture hall, theatre, library, museum, picture-gallery, and hospital.

The rest of the large space encircled by the 'Crystal Palace' is a public park, containing 145 acres, which includes ample recreation grounds within very easy access of all the people.

Running all round the Central Park (except where it is intersected by the boulevards) is a wide glass arcade called the 'Crystal Palace', opening on to the park. This building is in wet weather one of the favourite resorts of the people, whilst the knowledge that its bright shelter is ever close at hand tempts people into Central Park, even in the most doubtful of weathers. Here manufactured goods are exposed for sale, and here most of that class of shopping which requires the joy of deliberation and selection is done. The space enclosed by the Crystal Palace is, however, a good deal larger than is required for these purposes, and a considerable part of it is used as a Winter Garden —the whole forming a permanent exhibition of a most attractive character, whilst its circular form brings it near to every dweller in the town—the furthest removed inhabitant being within 600 yards.

Passing out of the Crystal Palace on our way to the outer ring of the town, we cross Fifth Avenue—lined, as are all the roads of the town, with trees—fronting which, and looking on to the Crystal Palace, we find a ring of very excellently built houses, each standing in its own ample grounds; and, as we continue our walk, we observe that the houses are for the most part built either in concentric rings, facing the various avenues (as the circular roads are termed), or fronting the boulevards and roads which all converge to the centre of the town. Asking the friend who accompanies us on our journey what the population of this little city may be, we are told about 30,000 in the city itself, and about 2,000 in the agricultural estate, and that there are in the town 5,500 building lots of an *average* size of 20 feet x 130 feet —the minimum space allotted for the purpose being 20 x 100. Noticing the very varied architecture and design which the houses and groups of houses display—some having common gardens and co-operative kitchens—we learn that general observance of street line or harmonious departure from it are the chief points as to house building, over which the municipal authorities exercise control, for, though proper sanitary arrangements are strictly enforced, the fullest measure of individual taste and preference is encouraged.

Walking still toward the outskirts of the town, we come upon 'Grand Avenue'. This avenue is fully entitled to the name it bears, for it is 420 feet wide,[1] and, forming a belt of green upwards of three miles long, divides that part of the town which lies outside Central Park into two belts. It really constitutes an additional park of 115 acres—a park which is within 240 yards of the furthest removed inhabitant. In this splendid avenue six sites, each of four acres, are occupied by public schools and their surrounding playgrounds and gardens, while other sites are reserved for churches, of such denominations as the religious beliefs of the people may determine, to be erected and maintained out of the funds of the worshippers and their friends. We observe that the houses fronting on Grand Avenue have departed (at least in one of the wards—that of which Diagram 3 is a representation)—from the general plan of concentric rings, and, in order to ensure a longer line of frontage on Grand Avenue, are arranged in crescents—thus also to the eye yet further enlarging the already splendid width of Grand Avenue.

On the outer ring of the town are factories, warehouses, dairies, markets, coal yards, timber yards, etc., all fronting on the circle railway, which encompasses the whole town, and which has sidings connecting it with a main line of railway which passes through the estate. This arrangement enables goods to be loaded direct into trucks from the warehouses and workshops, and so sent by railway to distant markets, or to be taken direct from the trucks into the warehouses or factories; thus not only effecting a very great saving in regard to packing and cartage, and reducing to a minimum loss from breakage, but also, by reducing the traffic on the roads of the town, lessening to a very marked extent the cost of their maintenance. The smoke fiend is kept well within bounds in Garden City; for all machinery is driven by electric energy, with the result that the cost of electricity for lighting and other purposes is greatly reduced.

The refuse of the town is utilized on the agricultural portions of the estate, which are held by various individuals in large farms, small holdings, allotments, cow pastures, etc.; the natural competition of these various methods of agriculture, tested by the willingness of occupiers to offer the highest rent

---

[1] Portland Place, London, is only 100 feet wide.

to the municipality, tending to bring about the best system of husbandry, or, what is more probable, the best *systems* adapted for various purposes. Thus it is easily conceivable that it may prove advantageous to grow wheat in very large fields, involving united action under a capitalist farmer, or by a body of co-operators; while the cultivation of vegetables, fruits, and flowers, which requires closer and more personal care, and more of the artistic and inventive faculty, may possibly be best dealt with by individuals, or by small groups of individuals having a common belief in the efficacy and value of certain dressings, methods of culture, or artificial and natural surroundings.

This plan, or, if the reader be pleased to so term it, this absence of plan, avoids the dangers of stagnation or dead level, and, though encouraging individual initiative, permits of the fullest co-operation, while the increased rents which follow from this form of competition are common or municipal property, and by far the larger part of them are expended in permanent improvements.

While the town proper, with its population engaged in various trades, callings, and professions, and with a store or depot in each ward, offers the most natural market to the people engaged on the agricultural estate, inasmuch as to the extent to which the townspeople demand their produce they escape altogether any railway rates and charges; yet the farmers and others are not by any means limited to the town as their only market, but have the fullest right to dispose of their produce to whomsoever they please. Here, as in every feature of the experiment, it will be seen that it is not the area of rights which is contracted, but the area of choice which is enlarged.

This principle of freedom holds good with regard to manufacturers and others who have established themselves in the town. These manage their affairs in their own way, subject, of course, to the general law of the land, and subject to the provision of sufficient space for workmen and reasonable sanitary conditions. Even in regard to such matters as water, lighting, and telephonic communication—which a municipality, if efficient and honest, is certainly the best and most natural body to supply—no rigid or absolute monopoly is sought; and if any private corporation or any body of individuals proved itself capable of supplying on more advantageous terms, either the whole town or a section of it, with these or any commodities the supply of which was taken up by the corporation, this would be allowed. No really sound system of *action* is in more need of artificial support than is any sound system of *thought*. The area of municipal and corporate action is probably destined to become greatly enlarged; but, if it is to be so, it will be because the people possess faith in such action, and that faith can be best shown by a wide extension of the area of freedom.

Dotted about the estate are seen various charitable and philanthropic institutions. These are not under the control of the municipality, but are supported and managed by various public-spirited people who have been invited by the municipality to establish these institutions in an open healthy district, and on land let to them at a pepper-corn rent, it occurring to the authorities that they can the better afford to be thus generous, as the spending power of these institutions greatly benefits the whole community. Besides, as those persons who migrate to the town are among its most energetic and resourceful members, it is but just and right that their more helpless brethren should be able to enjoy the benefits of an experiment which is designed for humanity at large.

Note: The following quotation appeared at the head of this chapter in the edition of 1898. *Ed.*

'No scene is continuously and untiringly loved, but one rich by joyful human labour; smooth in field; fair in garden; full in orchard; trim, sweet and frequent in homestead; ringing with voices of vivid existence. No air is sweet that is silent; it is only sweet when full of low currents of under sound—triplets of birds, and murmur and chirp of insects, and deep-toned words of men, and wayward trebles of childhood. As the art of life is learned, it will be found at last that all lovely things are also necessary;—the wild flower by the wayside, as well as the tended corn; and the wild birds and creatures of the forest, as well as the tended cattle; because man doth not live by bread only, but also by the desert manna; by every wondrous word and unknowable work of God.'—JOHN RUSKIN, *Unto This Last* (1862).

Chapter Two

The Revenue of Garden City, and how it is obtained—The Agricultural Estate

'It is my object to put forward a theoretical outline of a community so circumstanced and so maintained by the exercise of its own free will, guided by scientific knowledge, that the perfection of sanitary results will be approached, if not actually realized, in the coexistence of the lowest possible general mortality with the highest possible individual longevity.'—DR. B. W. RICHARDSON, *Hygeia; or, a City of Health* (1876).

'When drainage everywhere, with its double functions, restoring what it takes away, is accomplished, then, this being combined with the data of a new social economy, the products of the earth will be increased tenfold, and the problem of misery will be wonderfully diminished. Add the suppression of parasitism and it will be solved.'
—VICTOR HUGO, *Les Misérables* (1862).[1]

Amongst the essential differences between Garden City and other municipalities, one of the chief is its method of raising its revenue. Its entire revenue is derived from rents; and one of the purposes of this work is to show that the rents which may very reasonably be expected from the various tenants on the estate will be amply sufficient, if paid into the coffers of Garden City, (*a*) to pay the interest on the money with which the estate is purchased, (*b*) to provide a sinking fund for the purpose of paying off the principal, (*c*) to construct and maintain all such works as are usually constructed and maintained by municipal and other local authorities out of rates compulsorily levied, and (*d*) (after redemption of debentures) to provide a large surplus for other purposes, such as old-age pensions or insurance against accident and sickness.

Perhaps no difference between town and country is more noticeable than the difference in the rent charged for the use of

[1] These and several other quotations, which appeared in the original edition of 1898, were omitted from later editions. *Ed.*

the soil. Thus, while in some parts of London the rent is equal to £30,000 an acre, £4 an acre is an extremely high rent for agricultural land.[1] This enormous difference of rental value is, of course, almost entirely due to the presence in the one case and the absence in the other of a large population; and, as it cannot be attributed to the action of any particular individuals, it is frequently spoken of as the 'unearned increment', i.e. unearned by the landlord, though a more correct term would be 'collectively earned increment'.

The presence of a considerable population thus giving a greatly additional value to the soil, it is obvious that a migration of population on any considerable scale to any particular area will be certainly attended with a corresponding rise in the value of the land so settled upon, and it is also obvious that such increment of value may, with some foresight and pre-arrangement, become the property of the migrating people.

Such foresight and pre-arrangement, never before exercised in an effective manner, are displayed conspicuously in the case of Garden City, where the land, as we have seen, is vested in trustees, who hold it in trust (after payment of the debentures) for the whole community, so that the entire increment of value gradually created becomes the property of the municipality, with the effect that though rents may rise, and even rise considerably, such rise in rent will not become the property of private individuals, but will be applied in relief of rates. It is this arrangement which will be seen to give Garden City much of its magnetic power.

The site of Garden City we have taken to be worth at the time of its purchase £40 an acre, or £240,000. The purchase money may be assumed to represent thirty years' purchase, and on this basis the annual rent paid by the former tenants was £8,000. If, therefore, there was a population of 1,000 persons upon the estate at the time of the purchase, then each man, woman, and child was contributing towards this rent-roll an average sum of £8 per annum. But the population of Garden City, including its agricultural land, is, when completed, 32,000,

[1] These and all other figures are given as in the original edition of the book in 1898. Money values in England have of course changed considerably since that date. *Ed.*

and the estate has cost them a sum on which they pay an annual charge by way of interest of £9,600. Thus, while before the experiment was initiated, 1,000 persons out of their united earnings contributed £8,000 a year, or £8 *a head*, on the completion of the town 32,000 persons out of their united earnings will contribute £9,600 a year, or an average of *6s. a head*.

This sum of 6s. per head per annum is all the rent, strictly speaking, which the inhabitants of Garden City will ever be called upon to pay; for it is all the rent which they *pay away*, any further sum they pay being a contribution towards their rates.

Let us now suppose that each person, besides contributing annually 6s. a head, contributes an average annual sum of £1 14s., or £2 in all. In that case two things may be noticed. First, each person will be paying for ground rent and rates only one-fourth of the sum which each person before the purchase paid in ground rent alone; and, secondly, the Board of Management, after the payment of interest on the debentures, will receive an annual sum of £54,400, which, as will be presently shown, would, after providing a sinking fund (of £4,400), defray all those costs, charges, and expenses which are usually met by local taxation.

The average annual sum contributed by each man, woman, and child in England and Wales for local purposes is about £2 a head, and the average sum contributed for ground rent is, at a very low estimate, about £2 10s. The average yearly contribution for ground rent and local rates is, therefore, about £4 10s. It might, therefore, be safely assumed that the people of Garden City would willingly pay £2 per head in complete discharge of ground rent and local rates; but to make the case the clearer and stronger, we will test the supposed willingness of the tenants of Garden City to pay such a sum as £2 a year for rates and rents in another way.

For this purpose, let us deal first with the agricultural estate, leaving the town estate to be dealt with separately. Obviously the rent which can be secured will be considerably greater than before the town was built. Every farmer now has a market close to his doors. There are 30,000 townspeople to be fed. Those persons, of course, are perfectly free to get their foodstuffs from any part of the world, and in the case of many products will doubtless continue to be supplied from abroad. These farmers are hardly likely to supply them with tea, with coffee, with spices, with tropical fruits or with sugar,[1] and their struggle to compete with America and Russia for the supply of wheat or flour to the town may be as keen as ever. But surely the struggle will not be so despairing. A ray—a beam of hope will gladden the heart of the despairing home-producer of wheat, for while the American has to pay railway charges to the seaboard, charges for Atlantic transit and railway charges to the consumer, the farmer of Garden City has a market at his very doors, and this a market which the rent he contributes will help to build up.[2]

Or, consider vegetables and fruits. Farmers, except near towns, do not often grow them now. Why? Chiefly because of the difficulty and uncertainty of a market, and the high charges for freights and commission. To quote the words of Dr. Farquharson, M.P., when they 'try to dispose of these things they find themselves struggling so hopelessly in a spider's web of rings and middlemen, and speculators, that they are more than half-inclined to give up the attempt in despair, and fall back on those things that stand up straight and square to their prices in the open market'. A curious calculation may be interesting with regard to milk. Assuming each person in the town consumed only one-third of a pint a day, then 30,000 would consume 1,250 gallons a day, and might thus save, taking railway charges at a penny per gallon, upwards of £1,900 per annum in railway rates upon the one item of milk, a saving which must be multiplied by a large figure in order to realize the general saving to be effected by placing consumer and producer in such close association. In other words, the combination of town and country is not only healthful, but economic—a point which every step taken will serve to make yet more clear.

But the rents which the agricultural tenants of Garden City would be willing to pay would increase for another reason. The waste products of the town could, and this without heavy

[1] The electric light, with cheap motive power for its generation, with glass-houses, may make even some of these things possible.

[2] See *Fields, Factories, and Workshops*, by Prince Kropotkin (London, 1898), and *The Coming Revolution*, by Capt. J. W. Petavel.

charges for railway transport or other expensive agencies, be readily brought back to the soil, thus increasing its fertility. The question of sewage disposal is naturally a difficult one to deal with, but its inherent difficulty is often much increased by artificial and imperfect conditions already in existence. Thus, Sir Benjamin Baker, in his joint report with Mr. (now Sir) Alexander Binnie to the London County Council, says: 'In approaching the consideration of the vast question of the whole sewerage system of the Metropolis, and the state of the Thames, as a practical problem . . . we had clearly at once to recognize the fact that the general features of the main drainage system were unalterably settled, and must be accepted in the same way as the main lines of thoroughfares have to be accepted whether quite as we could wish them to be or not.' But on Garden City site, given the skilful engineer, he would have comparatively little difficulty. He would have, as it were, a clean sheet on which to prepare his plans, and the whole estate being equally the property of the municipality, he would have a free course before him, and would doubtless succeed in adding greatly to the productiveness of the agricultural estate.

The great increase in the number of allotments, especially such favourably situated allotments as are shown in Diagram 2, would also tend to raise the total sum offered in rent.

There are yet other reasons why the rent which a farmer on the Garden City estate would be willing to pay for his farm, or a labourer for his allotment, would tend to increase. The productiveness of the agricultural part of the estate, besides being increased by a well-devised system of sewage disposal, and by a new and somewhat extensive market, with unique conveniences for transit to more distant markets, would also be increased because the tenure on which the land is held encourages maximum cultivation. It is a just tenure. The agricultural portion of the estate is let at fair rents, with a right to continue in occupation as long as the tenant is willing to pay a rent equal to that offered by any would-be occupier, less, say, 10 per cent in favour of the occupying tenant—the incoming tenant having also to compensate the outgoing tenant for all unexhausted improvements. Under this system, while it would be impossible for the tenant to secure to himself any undue share of that natural increment of land-value which would be brought about by the general growth in well-being of the town, he would yet have, as all tenants in possession probably should have, a preference over any newcomer, and would know that he would not lose those fruits of his past industry which were not yet ingathered but were still adding their value to the soil. Surely no one can doubt that such a tenure would, of itself, tend greatly to increase at once the activity and industry of the tenant, the productivity of the soil, and the rent which the tenant would be willing to pay.

That there would be this increased offer of rent will become yet more obvious if we consider for a moment the *nature* of the rent paid by a tenant of Garden City. Part of what he pays would be in respect of interest on the debentures on which the money to purchase the estate was raised, or in the redemption of those debentures, and would thus, except so far as the debentures were held by residents on the estate, pass away from the community altogether; but the whole of the remaining sum paid would be expended locally, and the farmer would have a share equal to that of every adult in the administration of such money. The term 'rent', therefore, has, in Garden City, acquired a new meaning, and, for the sake of clearness, it will be necessary in future to use terms which will not be ambiguous. That part of the rent which represents interest on debentures will be hereafter called 'landlord's rent'; that part which represents repayment of purchase-money 'sinking fund'; that part which is devoted to public purposes 'rates'; while the total sum will be termed 'rate-rent'.

From these considerations, surely it is obvious that the '*rate-rent*' which the farmer will be willing to pay into the treasury of Garden City will be considerably higher than the *rent* he would be willing to pay to a private landlord, who, besides increasing his rent as the farmer makes his land more valuable, will also leave him with the full burden of local taxation resting upon him. In short the plan proposed embraces a system of sewage-disposal which will return to the soil in a transmuted form many of those products the growth of which, by exhausting its natural fertility, demand elsewhere the application of manures so expensive that the farmer becomes sometimes blinded to their necessity, and it also embraces a system of rate-rents by which many of the farmer's hard-earned sovereigns, hitherto lost to him by being paid away to his landlord, shall return to his exhausted exchequer, not indeed in the form in which they left it, but in a variety of useful forms, such as roads, schools, markets, which will assist him most materially, though indirectly, in his work, but which, under present conditions, entail so severe a burden as to make him naturally slow to see their inherent necessity, and even to look upon some of them with suspicion and dislike. Who can doubt that if the farm and the farmer can be placed under conditions so healthful and natural alike in a physical and moral sense, the willing soil and the hopeful farmer will alike respond to their new environment— the soil becoming more fertile by every blade of grass it yields, the farmer richer by every penny of rate-rent he contributes?

We are now in a position to see that the rate-rent which will be readily paid by farmer, small occupier, and allotment holder, would be considerably greater than the rent he paid before: (1) because of the presence of a new town population demanding new and more profitable farm products, in respect of which railway charges can be largely saved; (2) by the due return to the soil of its natural elements; (3) by the just, equitable, and natural conditions on which the land is held; and (4) by reason of the fact that the rent now paid is *rate and rent*, while the rent formerly paid left the rates to be paid by the tenant.

But certain as it is that the '*rate-rent*' would represent a very considerable increase over the bare *rent* formerly paid by the tenants on the estate, it is still very much a matter of conjecture what the 'rate-rent' would be; and we shall, therefore, be acting prudently if we greatly under-estimate the 'rate-rent' which would probably be offered. If, then, in view of all the circumstances, we estimate that the *farming population* of Garden City will be prepared to pay for rates and rent 50 per cent more than they before paid for *rent alone*, we shall reach the following result:

Estimated Gross Revenue from Agricultural Estate

Original rent paid by tenants of 5,000 acres, say	£6,500
Add 50 per cent for contributions to rates and sinking fund	3,250
Total 'rate-rent' from agricultural estate	£9,750

THE AGRICULTURAL ESTATE

We shall in the next chapter estimate the amount which may, on the most reasonable calculation, be expected from the town estate, and then proceed to consider the sufficiency of the total rate-rents for the municipal needs of the town.

Chapter Three

The Revenue of Garden City—Town Estate

'Whatever reforms be introduced into the dwellings of the London poor, it will still remain true that the whole area of London is insufficient to supply its population with fresh air and the free space that is wanted for wholesome recreation. A remedy for the overcrowding of London will still be wanted. . . . There are large classes of the population of London whose removal into the country would be in the long run economically advantageous; it would benefit alike those who moved and those who remained behind. . . . Of the 150,000 or more hired workers in the clothes-making trades, by far the greater part are very poorly paid, and do work which it is against all economic reason to have done where ground-rent is high.'
PROFESSOR MARSHALL, 'The Housing of the London Poor', *Contemporary Review*, 1884.

Having in the last chapter estimated the gross revenue which may be anticipated from the agricultural part of the estate at £9,750, we will now turn to the town estate (where, obviously, the conversion of an agricultural area into a town will be attended with a very large rise in land values), and endeavour roughly to estimate—again taking care to keep well within the mark—the amount of 'rate-rent' which will be freely offered by the tenants of the town estate.

The site of the town proper consists, it will be remembered, of 1,000 acres, and is assumed to have cost £40,000, the interest of which, at 4 per cent, is £1,600 per annum. This sum of £1,600 is, therefore, all the landlord's rent which the people of the town site will be called upon to pay, any additional 'rate-rent' they may contribute being devoted either to the payment of the purchase-money as 'sinking-fund', or applied as 'rates' to the construction and maintenance of roads, schools, water-works, and to other municipal purposes. It will be interesting, therefore, to see what sort of a burden 'landlord's rent' will represent per head, and what the community would secure by such contribution. Now, if the sum of £1,600, being the annual interest or 'landlord's rent', be divided by 30,000 (the supposed population of the town), it will be found to equal an annual contribution by each man, woman, and child of *rather less than 1s. 1d. per head*. This is all the 'landlord's rent' which will ever be levied, any additional sum collected as 'rate-rent' being applied to sinking-fund or to local purposes.

And now let us notice what this fortunately placed community obtains for this insignificant sum. It obtains for 1s. 1d. per head per annum, first, ample sites for homes, these averaging, as we have seen, 20 feet by 130 feet, and accommodating, on an average, 5½ persons to each lot. It obtains ample space for roads, some of which are of truly magnificent proportions, so wide and spacious that sunlight and air may freely circulate, and in which trees, shrubs, and grass give to the town a semi-rural appearance. It also obtains ample sites for town hall, public library, museum and picture gallery, theatre, concert hall, hospital, schools, churches, swimming baths, public markets, etc. It also secures a central park of 145 acres, and a magnificent avenue 420 feet wide, extending in a circle of over three miles, unbroken save by spacious boulevards and by schools and churches, which, one may be sure, will not be the less beautiful because so little money has been expended on their sites. It secures also all the land required for a railway 4½ miles long, encompassing the town; 82 acres for warehouses, factories, markets, and a splendid site for a Crystal Palace devoted to shopping, and serving also as a winter garden.

The leases under which all building sites are let do not, therefore, contain the usual covenant by the tenant to pay all rates, taxes, and assessments levied in respect of such property, but, on the contrary, contain a covenant by the landlord to apply the whole sum received, first, in payment of debenture interest; secondly, towards the redemption of the debentures; and thirdly, as to the whole of the balance, into a public fund, to be applied to public purposes, among these being the rates levied by public authorities, other than the municipal authority, of the city.

Let us now attempt to estimate the rate-rents which may be anticipated in respect of our town-estate.

First, we will deal with the home-building lots. All are excellently situated, but those fronting Grand Avenue (420 feet) and the magnificent boulevards (120 feet) would probably call forth the highest tenders. We can here deal only with averages, but we think anyone would admit that an average rate-rent of 6s. a foot frontage for home lots would be extremely moderate. *This would make the rate-rent of a building lot 20 feet wide in an average position £6 a year, and on this basis the 5,500 building lots would yield a gross revenue of £33,000.*

The rate-rents from the sites of factories, warehouses, markets, etc., cannot perhaps be so well estimated by the foot frontage, but we may perhaps safely assume that an average employer would willingly pay £2 in respect of each employee. It is, of course, not suggested that the rate-rent levied should be a poll-tax; it would, as has been said, be raised by competition among the tenants; but this way of estimating rate-rent to be paid will perhaps give a ready means by which manufacturers or other employers, co-operative societies, or individuals working on their own account, would be able to judge whether they would be lightly rated and rented as compared with their present position. It must be, however, distinctly borne in mind that we are dealing with *averages*; and if the figure should seem high to a large employer, it will seem ridiculously low to a small shopkeeper.

Now, in a town with a population of 30,000, there would be about twenty thousand persons between the ages of 16 and 65; and if it is assumed that 10,625 of these would be employed in factories, shops, warehouses, markets, etc., or in any way which involved the use of a site, other than a home-building site, to be leased from the municipality, there would be a revenue from this source of £21,250.

The gross revenue of the entire estate would therefore be:

Rate-rent from agricultural estate (see p. 64)	£9,750
Rate-rent from 5,500 home building lots at £6 per lot	33,000
Rate-rent from business premises, 10,625 persons employed at an average of £2 a head	21,250
	£64,000

Or £2 per head of population for rates and rent.

This sum would be available as follows:

TOWN ESTATE

For landlord's rent or interest on purchase money £240,000 at 4 per cent	£9,600
For sinking fund (thirty years)	4,400
For such purposes as are elsewhere defrayed out of rates	50,000
	£64,000

It is now important to inquire whether £50,000 will suffice for the municipal needs of Garden City.

Chapter Four

The Revenue of Garden City—General
Observations on its Expenditure

Before entering upon the question which presented itself at the conclusion of the last chapter—that of endeavouring to ascertain whether the estimated net available income of Garden City (£50,000 per annum) would be sufficient for its municipal needs, I will very shortly state how it is proposed to raise the money required for commencing operations. The money would be borrowed on 'B' debentures,[1] and would be secured by a charge upon the 'rate-rent', subject, of course, to the payment of interest and sinking fund in respect of the 'A' debentures on which the purchase money of the estate is raised. It is, perhaps, superfluous to remark that, though in the case of the land purchase it might be requisite to raise the whole, or at least some very considerable part of the purchase money before possession would be given of the estate, or operations upon it commenced, yet in regard to public works to be carried out upon the estate, the case is quite different, and it would be by no means necessary or advisable to defer the commencement of operations until the whole sum which might be ultimately required should be raised. Probably no town was ever built on such onerous conditions as would be involved in the raising at the outset of such a very considerable sum as would defray the cost of all its public works; and though the circumstances under which Garden City is to be built may be unique, there is, as will by and by be seen, not only no need for making an exception of the town in respect of initial capital, but quite exceptional reasons will become more and more apparent which make the overlaying of the enterprise with superabundant capital altogether unnecessary, and therefore inexpedient; although, of course, there must be a sufficient sum to enable all real economies to be readily effected.

[1] See note on page 50.

Perhaps it may be well in this connection to draw a distinction as to the amount of capital required between the case of the building of a town and the building, let us say, of a large iron bridge across an estuary. In the case of the bridge it is highly expedient to raise the entire sum required before commencing operations, for the simple reason that the bridge is not a bridge until the last rivet is driven home, nor, until its entire completion and its connection with the railways or roadways at either end, has it any revenue-earning power. Except, therefore, on the assumption that it is to be fully completed, it offers very little security for the capital sunk upon it. Hence it would be very natural for those who are asked to invest to say, 'We will not put any money into this enterprise until you show us that you can get enough to complete it.' But the money which it is proposed to raise for the development of Garden City site leads to speedy results. It is to be expended upon roads, schools, etc. These works will be carried out with due regard to the number of lots which have been let to tenants, who undertake to build as from a certain date; and, therefore, the money expended will very soon begin to yield a return in the shape of a rate-rent, representing, in reality, a greatly improved ground rent; when those who have advanced money on the 'B' debentures will have a really first-class security, and further sums should be easily obtainable, and at a reduced rate of interest. Again, it is an important part of the project that each ward, or one-sixth part of the city,[1] should be in some sense a complete town by itself, and thus the school buildings might serve, in the earlier stages, not only as schools, but as places for religious worship, for concerts, for libraries, and for meetings of various kinds, so that all outlay on expensive municipal and other buildings might be deferred until the later stages of the enterprise. Work, too, would be practically completed in one ward before commencing on another, and the operations in the various wards would be taken up in due and proper sequence, so that those portions of the town site on which building operations were not in progress would also be a source of revenue, either as allotments, cow-pastures, or, perhaps, as brickfields.

[1] See Diagram 3.

Let us now deal with the subject immediately before us. Will the principles on which Garden City is to be built have any bearing on the effectiveness of its municipal expenditure? In other words, will a given revenue yield greater results than under ordinary conditions? These questions will be answered in the affirmative. It will be shown that, pound for pound, money will be more effectively spent than elsewhere, and that there will be many great and obvious economies which cannot be expressed in figures with much accuracy, but which would certainly represent in the aggregate a very large sum.

The first great economy to be noticed is that the item of 'landlord's rent', which, under ordinary conditions, largely enters into municipal expenditure, will, in Garden City, scarcely enter at all. Thus, all well-ordered towns require administrative buildings, schools, swimming baths, libraries, parks; and the sites which these and other corporate undertakings occupy are usually purchased. In such cases the money necessary for the purchase of the sites is generally borrowed on the security of the rates; and thus it is that a very considerable part of the total rates levied by a municipality are ordinarily applied, not to productive works, but either to what we have termed 'landlord's rent', in the shape of interest on money borrowed to effect the purchase, or to the provision of a sinking fund in payment of the purchase money of the land so acquired, which is landlord's rent in a capitalized form.

Now, in Garden City, all such expenditure, with such exceptions as road sites on the agricultural estate, has been already provided for. Thus, the 250 acres for public parks, the sites for schools and other public buildings, will cost the ratepayers nothing whatever, or, to put it more correctly, their cost, which was really £40 per acre, has been covered, as we have seen, by the annual average contribution of 1s. 1d. per head, which each person is supposed to make in discharge of landlord's rent; and the revenue of the town, £50,000, is the *net* revenue after all interest and sinking fund in respect of the whole site has been deducted. In considering, therefore, the question whether £50,000 is a sufficient revenue, it must be remembered that in no case has any cost of municipal sites to be first deducted from that amount.

Another item in which a great economy will be effected will be found in a comparison between Garden City and any old city like London. London wishes to breathe a fuller municipal spirit, and so proceeds to construct schools, to pull down slums, to erect libraries, swimming baths, etc. In these cases, it has not only to purchase the freeholds of the sites, but also has usually to pay for the buildings which had been previously erected thereon, and which are purchased solely, of course, with a view to their demolition and to a clearing of the ground, and frequently it has also to meet claims for business-disturbance, together with heavy legal expenses in settling claims. In this connection it may be remarked that the inclusive cost of *sites* of schools purchased by the London School Board since its constitution, i.e. the cost, including old buildings, business-disturbance, law charges, etc., has already reached the enormous sum of £3,516,072,[1] and the exclusive cost of the sites (370 acres in extent) ready for building by the Board is equal, on the average, to £9,500 per acre.[2]

At this rate the cost of the 24 acres[3] of school sites for Garden City would be £228,000, so that another site for a model city could be purchased out of what would be saved in Garden City in respect of school sites alone. 'Oh, but,' it may be said, 'the school sites of Garden City are extravagantly large, and would be out of the question in London, and it is altogether unfair to compare a small town like Garden City with London, the wealthy capital of a mighty Empire.' I would reply, 'It is quite

[1] See Report, London School Board, 6th May 1897, p. 1,480.

[2] 'It is a great pity that the old suggestion of attaching, wherever possible, half an acre or so of land to each public elementary school in the country has never been carried out. School gardens might be made the means of giving the young an insight into horticulture, the effect of which they would find pleasant and profitable in after life. The physiology and relative value of food is a much more useful branch of school instruction than many a branch upon which the young have wasted years of their time, and the school garden would be the most valuable of object lessons.' *The Echo*, Nov. 1890.

[3] Since Howard wrote, the area considered necessary for schools has much increased. For primary schools alone a population of 30,000 now needs fifty-one acres (*Housing Manual 1944*) and for schools of all types about 140 acres. *Ed.*

true that the cost of land in London would make such sites extravagant, not to say prohibitive—they would cost about £40,000,000 sterling—but does not this of itself suggest a most serious defect of system, and that at a most vital part? Can children be better taught where land costs £9,500 an acre than where it costs £40? Whatever may be the real economic value of the London site, for other purposes—as to which we may have something to say at a later stage—for school purposes, wherein lies the advantage that the sites on which its schools are built are frequently surrounded by dingy factories or crowded courts and alleys? If Lombard Street is an ideal place for banks, is not a park like the Central Avenue of Garden City an ideal place for schools?—and is not the welfare of our children the primary consideration with any well-ordered community? 'But', it may be said, 'the children must be educated near their homes, and these homes must be near the places where their parents work.' Precisely; but does not the scheme provide for this in the most effective manner, and in that respect also are not the school sites of Garden City superior to those of London? The children will have to expend less than an average amount of energy in going to school, a matter, as all educationists admit, of immense importance, especially in the winter. But further, have we not heard from Professor Marshall (see heading to Chapter Three) that '150,000 people, in London, engaged in the clothes-making trades, are doing work which it is against all economic reason to have done where ground rent is high'—in other words, that these 150,000 people *should not be in London at all*; and does not the consideration that the education of the children of such workers is carried on at once under inferior conditions and at enormous cost add weight and significance to the Professor's words? If these workers ought not to be in London, then their homes, for which, insanitary as they are, they pay heavy rents, ought not to be in London; a certain proportion of the shop-keepers who supply their wants should not be in London; and various other people to whom the wages earned by these persons in the clothes-making trade give employment should not be in London. Hence, there is a sense—and a very real one—in which it *is* fair to compare the cost of school sites in Garden City with the cost of school sites in London; because obviously if these people do, as suggested by Professor Marshall, migrate from London, they can at once effect (if they make, as I have suggested, proper provision beforehand) not only a great saving in respect of ground rent for their workshops, but also a vast saving in respect of sites for homes, schools, and other purposes; and this saving is obviously the difference between what is now paid and what would be paid under the new conditions, minus the loss incurred (if any), and plus the numerous gains secured as the result of such removal.

Let us for the sake of clearness make the comparison in another way. The people of London have paid a capital sum representing, when spread over the whole population of London (this being taken at 6,000,000), upwards of 11s. 6d. per head of population for school sites held by the London School Board, a sum which is, of course, exclusive of the sites for voluntary schools. The population of Garden City, 30,000 in number, have entirely saved that 11s. 6d. per head, making a total saving of £17,250, which at 3 per cent involves an annual saving of £517 in perpetuity. And besides thus saving £517 a year as interest on cost of sites for schools, Garden City has secured sites for its schools incomparably better than those of London schools—sites which afford ample accommodation for all the children of the town, and not, as in the case of the London School Board, accommodation for only half of the children of the municipality. (The sites of the London School Board are 370 acres in extent, or about 1 acre to every 16,000 of the population, while the people of Garden City have obtained 24 acres or 1 acre for every 1,250.) In other words, Garden City secures sites which are larger, better placed, and in every way more suitable for educational purposes, at a mere fraction of the cost which in London is incurred for sites vastly inferior in every respect.

The economies with which we have thus dealt are, it will be seen, effected by the two simple expedients we have referred to. First, by buying the land *before* a new value is given to it by migration, the migrating people obtain a site at an extremely low figure, and secure the coming increment for themselves and those who come after them; and secondly, by coming to a new site, they do not have to pay large sums for old buildings, for compensation for disturbance, and for heavy legal charges. The practicability of securing for the poor workers of London the first of these great advantages appears to have been for the moment overlooked by Professor Marshall in his article in the *Contemporary Review*,[1] for the Professor remarks 'Ultimately all would gain by the migration, *but most*' (the italics are my own) '*the landowners and the railroads connected with the colony.*' Let us then adopt the expedient here advocated of securing that the *landowners*, '*who . . . will gain most*' by a project specially designed to benefit a class now low down in the social scale, *shall be those very people themselves*, as members of a new municipality, and then a strong additional inducement will be held out to them to make a change, which nothing but the lack of combined effort has hitherto prevented. As to the benefit to be derived by the railways, while no doubt the building up of the town would specially benefit the main line of railway which passed through the estate, it is also true that the earnings of the people would not be diminished to the usual extent by railway freights and charges. (See Chapter Two, also Chapter Five, p. 84.)

We now come to deal with an element of economy which will be simply incalculable. This is to be found in the fact that the town is definitely planned, so that the whole question of municipal administration may be dealt with by one far-reaching scheme. It is not by any means necessary, and it is not, humanly speaking, possible, that the final scheme should be the work of one mind. It will no doubt be the work of many minds—the minds of engineers, of architects and surveyors, of landscape gardeners and electricians. But it is essential, as we have said, that there should be unity of design and purpose—that the town should be planned as a whole, and not left to grow up in a chaotic manner as has been the case with all English towns, and more or less so with the towns of all countries. A town, like a flower, or a tree, or an animal, should, at each stage of its growth, possess unity, symmetry, completeness, and the effect of growth should never be to destroy that unity, but to give it greater purpose, nor to mar that symmetry, but to make it more

[1] No one is, of course, better aware of this possibility than the Professor himself. (See *Principles of Economics*, 2nd ed., Bk. V, Chaps. x and xiii.)

symmetrical; while the completeness of the early structure should be merged in the yet greater completeness of the later development.[1]

Garden City is not only planned, but it is planned with a view to the very latest of modern requirements,[2] and it is obviously always easier, and usually far more economical and completely satisfactory, to make out of fresh material a new instrument than to patch up and alter an old one. This element of economy will be perhaps best dealt with by a concrete illustration, and one of a very striking nature at once presents itself.

In London the question of building a new street between

[1] It is commonly thought that the cities of the United States are planned. This is only true in a most inadequate sense. American towns certainly do not consist of intricate mazes of streets, the lines of which would appear to have been sketched out by cows: and a few days' residence in any American city except a few of the oldest, will ordinarily enable one to find his way about it; but there is, notwithstanding, little real design, and that of the crudest character. Certain streets are laid out, and as the city grows, these are extended and repeated in rarely broken monotony. Washington is a magnificent exception as to the laying out of its streets; but even this city is not designed with a view of securing to its people ready access to nature, while its parks are not central, nor are its schools and other buildings arranged in a scientific manner.

[2] 'London has grown up in a chaotic manner, without any unity of design, and at the chance discretion of any persons who were fortunate enough to own land as it came into demand at successive periods for building operations. Sometimes a great landlord laid out a quarter in a manner to tempt the better class of residents by squares, gardens, or retired streets, often cut off from through traffic by gates and bars; but even in these cases London as a whole has not been thought of, and no main arteries have been provided for. In other and more frequent cases of small landowners, the only design of builders has been to crowd upon the land as many streets and houses as possible, regardless of anything around them, and without open spaces or wide approaches. A careful examination of a map of London shows how absolutely wanting in any kind of plan has been its growth, and how little the convenience and wants of the whole population or the considerations of dignity and beauty have been consulted.' Right Hon. G. J. Shaw-Lefevre, *New Review*, 1891, p. 435.

Holborn and the Strand has been for many years under consideration, and at length a scheme is being carried out, imposing an enormous cost on the people of London. 'Every such change in the street geography of London displaces thousands of the poor'—I quote from the *Daily Chronicle* of 6th July 1898—'and for many years all public or quasi-public schemes have been charged with the liability to rehouse as many of them as possible. This is as it should be; but the difficulty begins when the public is asked to face the music and pay the bill. In the present case some three thousand souls of the working population have to be turned out. After some searching of heart, it is decided that most of them are so closely tied to the spot by their employment that it would be a hardship to send them more than a mile away. The result, in cash, is that London must spend in rehousing them about £100 a head—or £300,000 in all. As to those who cannot fairly be asked to go even a mile away—hangers-on to the market, or others tethered to the spot—the cost will be even higher. They will require to have parcels of the precious land cleared by the great scheme itself, and the result of that will be to house them at the handsome figure of £260 apiece, or some £1,400 for every family of five or six. Financial statements convey little to the ordinary mind. Let us make it a little more intelligible. A sum of £1,400 means, in the house market, a rental of nearly £100 a year. It would buy an excellent in fact a sumptuous, house and garden at Hampstead, such as the better middle-class delight in. It would purchase anywhere in the nearer suburbs such houses as men with £1,000 a year inhabit. If one went further afield, to the new neighbourhoods which the City clerk can easily reach by rail, a £1,400 house represents actual magnificence.' But on what scale of comfort will the poor Covent Garden labourer with a wife and four children live? The £1,400 will by no means represent a fair standard of comfort, to say nothing of magnificence. 'He will live in three rooms sufficiently small in a block at least three storeys high.' Contrast this with what might be done on a new area, by carefully planning a bold scheme at the outset. Streets of greater width than this new street would be laid out and constructed at a mere fraction of the cost, while a sum of £1,400, instead of providing one family with 'three rooms sufficiently small in

78

blocks at least three storeys high', would provide seven families in Garden City with a comfortable six-roomed cottage each, and with a nice little garden; and, manufacturers being concurrently induced to build on the sites set apart for them, each breadwinner would be placed within easy walking distance of his work.[1]

There is another modern need which all towns and cities should be designed to meet—a need which has arisen with the evolution of modern sanitation, and which has of recent years been accentuated by the rapid growth of invention. Subways for sewerage and surface drainage, for water, gas, telegraph and telephone wires, electric lighting wires, wires for conveying motive power, pneumatic tubes for postal purposes, have come to be regarded as economic if not essential. But if they would be a source of economy in an old city, how much more so in new ones; for on a clean sheet it will be easy to use the very best appliances for their construction, and to avail ourselves to the fullest extent of the ever-growing advantages which they possess as the number of services which they accommodate increases. Before the subways can be constructed, trenches somewhat wide and deep must be excavated. In making these the most approved excavating machinery could be employed. In old towns this might be very objectionable, if not, indeed, quite impossible. But here, in Garden City, the steam navvy would not make its appearance in the parts where people were living, but where they were coming to live after its work in preparing the way had been completed. What a grand thing it would be if the people of England could, by an actual illustration under their very eyes, be convinced that machinery can be so used as to confer not only an ultimate national benefit, but a direct and immediate advantage, and that not only upon those who actually own it or use it, but on others who are given work by its magic aid. What

[1] The great Kingsway street improvement scheme (1900–10) cost over £4,000,000. After crediting receipts, the net cost to the London rates up to 1956 is estimated at £3,500,000. By 1986 it is expected that this will be written off out of revenue (Dr. W. A. Robson, *Government and Misgovernment of London*, 1939). But this cheerful calculation of course ignores loss of interest on the ratepayers' huge 'investment'. *Ed.*

a happy day it would be for the people of this country, and of all countries, if they could learn, from practical experience, that machinery can be used on an extended scale to *give* employment as well as *to take it away*—to *implace* labour as well as to *displace* it—to free men as well as to *enslave* them. There will be plenty of work to be done in Garden City. That is obvious. It is also obvious that, until a large number of houses and factories are built, many of these things cannot be done, and that the faster the trenches are dug, the subways finished, the factories and the houses built, and the light and the power turned on, the sooner can this town, the home of an industrious and a happy people, be built, and the sooner can others start the work of building other towns, not like it, but gradually becoming as much superior to it as our present locomotives are to the first crude attempts of the pioneers of mechanical traction.

We have now shown four cogent reasons why a given revenue should, in Garden City, yield vastly greater results than under ordinary conditions.

(1) That no 'landlord's rent' or interest in respect of freeholds would be payable other than the small amount which has been already provided for in estimating net revenue.

(2) That the site being practically clear of buildings and other works, but little expenditure would be incurred in the purchase of such buildings, or compensation for business-disturbance, or legal and other expenses in connection therewith.

(3) The economy arising out of a definite plan, and one in accordance with modern needs and requirements, thus saving those items of expenditure which are incurred in old cities as it is sought to bring them into harmony with modern ideas.

(4) The possibility, as the whole site will be clear for operations, of introducing machinery of the very best and most modern type in road-making and other engineering operations.

There are other economies which will become apparent to the reader as he proceeds, but, having cleared the ground by discussing general principles, we shall be better prepared to discuss the question as to the sufficiency of our estimates in another chapter.

Chapter Five

Further Details of Expenditure on Garden City

'Oh! if those who rule the destinies of nations would but remember this—if they would but think how hard it is for the very poor to have engendered in their hearts that love of home from which all domestic virtues spring, when they live in dense and squalid masses, where social decency is lost, or rather never found—if they would but turn aside from the wide thoroughfares and great houses, and strive to improve the wretched dwellings in bye-ways, where only Poverty may walk,—many low roofs would point more truly to the sky, than the loftiest steeple that now rears proudly up from the midst of guilt, and crime, and horrible disease, to mock them by its contrast. In hollow voices from Workhouse, Hospital, and Jail, this truth is preached from day to day, and has been proclaimed for years. It is no light matter—no outcry from the working vulgar—no mere question of the people's health and comforts that may be whistled down on Wednesday nights. In love of home, the love of country has its rise; and who are the truer patriots or the better in time of need—those who venerate the land, owning its wood, and stream, and earth, and all that they produce, or those who love their country, boasting not a foot of ground in all its wide domain?'—CHARLES DICKENS, *The Old Curiosity Shop* (1841).

To make this chapter interesting to the general reader would be difficult, perhaps impossible; but if carefully studied, it will, I think, be found to abundantly establish one of the main propositions of this book—that the rate-rent of a well-planned town, built on an agricultural estate, will amply suffice for the creation and maintenance of such municipal undertakings as are usually provided for out of rates compulsorily levied.

The net available revenue of Garden City, after payment of interest on debentures, and providing a sinking fund for the landed estate, has been already estimated at £50,000 per annum (see Chapter Three, p. 69). Having, in the fourth chapter, given special reasons why a given expenditure in Garden City would be unusually productive, I will now enter into fuller details, so that any criticism which this book may elicit, having something tangible to deal with, may be the more valuable in preparing the ground for an experiment such as is here advocated.

		EXPENDITURE	
		On Capital Account	On Maintenance and Working Expenses
See Note			
(A)	25 miles roads (city) at £4,000 a mile	£100,000	£2,500
(B)	6 miles additional roads, country estate at £1,200	7,200	350
(C)	Circular railway and bridges, 5½ miles at £3,000	16,500	1,500
(D)	Schools for 6,400 children, or one-fifth of the total population, at £12 per school place for capital account, and £3 maintenance, etc.	76,800	(maintenance only) 19,200
(E)	Town Hall	10,000	2,000
(F)	Library	10,000	600
(G)	Museum	10,000	600
(H)	Parks, 250 acres at £50	12,500	1,250
(I)	Sewage disposal	20,000	1,000
		£263,000	£29,000
(K)	Interest on £263,000 at 4½ per cent		11,835
(L)	Sinking Fund to provide for extinction of debt in thirty years		4,480
(M)	Balance available for rates levied by local bodies within the area of which the estate is situated		4,685
			£50,000

Besides the above expenditure, a considerable outlay would be incurred in respect of markets, water supply, lighting, tramways, and other revenue-yielding undertakings. But these items of expenditure are almost invariably attended with considerable profits, which go in aid of rates. No calculation, therefore, need be made in respect of these.

I will now deal separately with most of the items in the above estimate.

(A) Roads and Streets

The first point to be observed under this head is that the cost of making new streets to meet the growth of population is generally not borne by the ground landlord nor defrayed out of the rates. It is usually paid by the building-owner before the local authorities will consent to take the road over as a free gift. It is obvious, therefore, that the greater part of the £100,000 *might* be struck out. Experts will also not forget that the cost of the road sites is elsewhere provided for. In considering the question of the actual sufficiency of the estimate, they will also remember that of the boulevards one-half and of the streets and avenues one-third may be regarded as in the nature of park, and the cost of laying out and maintenance of these portions of the roads is dealt with under the head 'Parks'. They will also note that road-making materials would probably be found near at hand, and that, the railway relieving the streets of most of the heavy traffic, the more expensive methods of paving need not be resorted to. The cost, £4,000 per mile, would, however, be doubtless inadequate if subways are constructed, as probably they ought to be. The following consideration, however, has led me not to estimate for these. Subways are, where useful, a source of economy. The cost of maintaining roads is lessened, as the continual breaking-up for laying and repairing of water, gas, and electric mains is avoided, while any waste from leaky pipes is quickly detected, and thus the subways *pay*. Their cost should, therefore, be debited rather to cost of water, gas, and electric supplies, and these services are almost invariably a source of revenue to the Company or Corporation which constructs them.

(B) Country Roads

These roads are only forty feet wide, and £1,200 a mile is ample. The cost of sites has in this case to be defrayed out of estimate.

(C) Circular Railway and Bridges

The cost of site is elsewhere provided for (see p. 67). The cost of maintenance does not, of course, include working expenses, locomotives, etc. To cover these a charge based on cost might be made to traders using the line. It should also be noticed that, as in the case of roads, by showing that the expense of this undertaking could be defrayed out of the rate-rent, I am proving more than I undertook to prove. I am proving that the rate-rent is sufficient to provide for landlords' rent, for such purposes as are usually defrayed out of rent, *and also for greatly extending the area of municipal activity.*

It may here be well to point out that this circle railway not only will save the trader the expense of carting to and from his warehouse or factory, but will enable him to claim a rebate from the railway company. Section 4 of the Railway and Canal Tariff Act, 1894, enacts: 'Whenever merchandise is received or delivered by a railway company at any siding or branch railway not belonging to the company, and a dispute arises between the railway company and the consignor or consignee of such merchandise, as to any allowance or rebate from the rates charged to such consignor or consignee, in respect that the railway company does not provide station accommodation or perform terminal services, the Railway and Canal Commissioners shall have jurisdiction to hear and determine what, if any, is a just and reasonable allowance or rebate.'

(D) Schools

This estimate of £12 per school place represents what was only a few years ago (1892) the average cost per child of the London School Board for building, architect, and clerk of the works, and for furniture and fittings; and no one can doubt that buildings greatly superior to those in London could be obtained for this sum. The saving in sites has been already dealt with, but it may be remarked that in London the cost per child for sites has been £6 11s. 10d.

As showing how ample this estimate is, it may be observed that the cost of schools which have been proposed to be built by a private company at Eastbourne, 'with a view of keeping out the School Board', is estimated at £2,500 for 400 places, or but little more than half the sum per school place provided in the estimate for Garden City.

The cost of maintenance, £3 per head, is probably sufficient, in view of the fact that the 'expenditure per scholar in actual average attendance' in England and Wales, as given in the Report of the Committee of Council on Education, 1896–7, c. 8545, is £2 11s. 11½d. It must be especially noticed, too, that the whole cost of education is, in these estimates, assumed to be borne by Garden City, though a considerable part would be, in the ordinary course, borne by the National Exchequer. The amount of income per scholar in actual average attendance in England and Wales, as given in the same report, is £1 1s. 2d. as against a rate in Garden City of £3. So that I am again, in the case of the schools, as in the case of roads and circle railway, proving more than I set out to prove.

(E) Town Hall and Expenses of Management
It is to be noticed that the estimates of the various undertakings are intended to cover professional direction and supervision of architects, engineers, teachers, etc. The £2,000 for maintenance and working expenses under this head is, therefore, intended to include only the salaries of town clerk and of officials other than those comprised under special heads, together with incidental expenses.

(F) Library, and (G) Museum
The latter is usually and the former not infrequently elsewhere provided for out of funds other than rates. So, here again, I am more than proving my case.

(H) Parks and Road Ornamentation
This item of cost would not be incurred until the undertaking was in a thoroughly sound financial condition, and the park space for a considerable period might be a source of revenue as agricultural land. Further, much of the park space would probably be left in a state of nature. Forty acres of this park space is road ornamentation, but the planting of trees and shrubs would not entail great expense. Again, a considerable part of

the area would be reserved for cricket-fields, lawn-tennis courts, and other playgrounds, and the clubs using public grounds might perhaps be called upon to contribute to the expense of keeping these in order, as is customary elsewhere.

(I) Sewage Disposal

All that need be said on this subject has been said in Chapter One, p. 55, and Chapter Two, pp. 61–2.

(K) Interest

The money to construct the public works with which we have been dealing is supposed to be borrowed at $4\frac{1}{2}$ per cent. The question here arises—a question partly dealt with in Chapter Four—what is the security for those who lend money on the 'B' debentures?

My answer is threefold.

(1) Those who advance money to effect any improvements on land have a security the safety of which is in reality largely determined by the effectiveness with which the money so advanced is spent; and, applying this truism, I venture to say that, for effectiveness of expenditure, no money which the investing public has been for many years asked to subscribe for improvements of a like nature has an equal security, whether it be measured by miles of road, acres of park, or numbers of school children well provided for.

(2) Those who advance money to effect improvements on land have a security the safety of which is largely determined by the consideration, aye or no, are other and yet more valuable works to be simultaneously carried out by others at their own expense, which other works are to become a security in respect of the first-mentioned advance; and, applying this second truism, I say that, as the money for effecting the public improvements here described would only be asked for as and when other improvements—factories, houses, shops, etc. (costing far more money than the public works necessary at any given period)— were about to be built or were in process of building, the quality of the security would be a very high one.

(3) It is difficult to name a better security than that offered when money is to be expended in converting an agricultural estate into an urban, and this of the very best known type.

That the scheme is in reality a 3 per cent security, and would in its later stages become so, I entertain little doubt; but I do not forget that, though its points of novelty are the very elements which really *make* it secure, they may not make it *seem* so, and that those who are merely looking out for an investment may eye it with some distrust because of its novelty. We shall have in the first instance to look to those who will advance money with somewhat mixed motives—public spirit, love of enterprise, and possibly, as to some persons, with a lurking belief that they will be able to dispose of their debentures at a premium, as they probably will. Therefore, I put down 4½ per cent, but if anyone's conscience prick him he may tender at 2 or 2½, or may even advance money without interest.

(L) Sinking Fund

This sinking fund, which provides for the extinction of the debt in thirty years, compares most favourably with that usually provided by local bodies for works of so permanent a character. The Local Government Board frequently allows loans to be created with a sinking fund extending over much longer periods. It is to be remembered also that an additional sinking fund for the landed estate has been already provided (see Chapter Four, p. 70).

(M) Balance available for Rates levied by Local Bodies within whose jurisdiction the estate is situated

It will be seen that the whole scheme of Garden City will make extremely few demands upon the resources of outside local authorities. Roads, sewers, schools, parks, libraries, etc., will be provided out of the funds of the new 'municipality', and in this way the whole scheme will come to the agriculturists at present on the estate very much like 'a rate in aid'; for, as rates are only raised for the purpose of public expenditure, it follows that, there being little or no fresh call upon the rates while the number of ratepayers is greatly increased, the rate per head must fall. I do not, however, forget that there are some functions which such a voluntary organization as Garden City could not take over, such as the police and the administration of the poor-law. As to the latter, it is believed that the whole scheme will in the long run make such rates unnecessary, as Garden City will provide, at all events from the time when the estate has been fully paid for, pensions for all its needy old citizens. Meantime and from the very outset it is doing its full share of charitable work. It has allotted sites of 30 acres for various institutions, and at a later stage will doubtless be prepared to assume the whole cost of maintaining them.

With regard to police rates, it is not believed that these can be largely increased by the coming into the town of 30,000 citizens, who, for the most part, will be of the law-abiding class; for, there being but one landlord, and this the community, it will not be difficult to prevent the creation of those surroundings which make the intervention of the police so frequently necessary. (See Chapter Seven.)

I have, I think, now fully established my contention that the rate-rent which would be willingly offered by the tenants of Garden City, in respect of the advantages afforded them, would be amply sufficient: (1) to pay landlord's rent in the form of interest on debentures; (2) to provide a sinking fund for the entire abolition of landlord's rent; and (3) to provide for the municipal needs of the town without recourse to any Act of Parliament for the enforcement of rates—the community depending solely on the very large powers it possesses as a landlord.

(N) Revenue-bearing Expenditure

If the conclusion already arrived at—that the experiment advocated affords an outlet for an extremely effective expenditure of labour and capital—is sound in regard to objects the cost of which is usually defrayed out of rates, that conclusion must, I think, be equally sound in regard to tramways, lighting, water-supply, and the like, which, when carried on by municipalities, are usually made a source of revenue, thus relieving the rate-payer by making his rates lighter. And as I have added nothing to the proposed revenue for any prospective profits on such undertakings, I do not propose to make any estimate of expenditure.

Chapter Six

Administration

'The present evils of city life are temporary and remediable. The abolition of the slums, and the destruction of their virus, are as feasible as the drainage of a swamp, and the total dissipation of its miasmas. The conditions and circumstances that surround the lives of the masses of the people in modern cities can be so adjusted to their needs as to result in the highest development of the race, in body, in mind and in moral character. The so-called problems of the modern city are but the various phases of the one main question: How can the environment be most perfectly adapted to the welfare of urban populations? And science can meet and answer every one of these problems. The science of the modern city—of the ordering of the common concerns in dense population groups—draws upon many branches of theoretical and practical knowledge. It includes administrative science, statistical science, engineering and technological science, sanitary science, and educational, social and moral science. If one uses the term City Government in the large sense that makes it inclusive of this entire ordering of the general affairs and interests of the community, and, further, if one grasps the idea that the cheerful and rational acceptance of urban life as a great social fact demands that the City Government should proceed to make such urban life conduce positively to the welfare of all the people whose lawful interests bring them together as denizens of great towns, he will understand the point of view from which this book had been written.'—ALBERT SHAW, *Municipal Government in Great Britain* (1895).

I have in the fourth and fifth chapters dealt with the fund at the disposal of the Board of Management, and have endeavoured to show, and I believe with success, that the rate-rents collected by the trustees in their capacity of landlords of the towns will suffice: (1) to provide interest on the debentures with which the estate is purchased; (2) to provide a sinking fund which will at a comparatively early date leave the community free from the burden of interest on such debentures, and (3) to enable the Board of Management to carry on such undertakings

89

as are elsewhere, for the most part, carried out by means of rates compulsorily levied.

A most important question now arises regarding the extent to which municipal enterprise is to be carried, and how far it is to supersede private enterprise. We have already by implication stated that the experiment advocated does not involve, as has been the case in so many social experiments—the complete municipalization of industry and the elimination of private enterprise. But what principle is to guide us in determining the line which shall separate municipal from private control and management? Mr. Joseph Chamberlain has said: 'The true field for municipal activity is limited to those things which the community can do better than the individual.' Precisely, but that is a truism, and does not carry us one whit further, for the very question at issue is as to *what those things are* which the community can do better than the individual; and when we seek for an answer to this question we find two directly conflicting views —the view of the socialist, who says: Every phase of wealth-production and distribution can be best performed by the community; and the view of the individualist, who contends these things are best left to the individual. But probably the true answer is to be found at neither extreme, is only to be gained by experiment, and will differ in different communities and at different periods. With a growing intelligence and honesty in municipal enterprise, with greater freedom from the control of the Central Government, it may be found—especially on municipally owned land—that the field of municipal activity may grow so as to embrace a very large area, and yet the municipality claim no rigid monopoly and the fullest rights of combination exist.

Bearing this in mind, the municipality of Garden City will, at the outset, exercise great caution, and not attempt too much. The difficulty of raising the necessary funds with which to carry on municipal undertakings would be greatly increased if the Board of Management attempted to do everything; and, in the prospectus to be ultimately issued, a clear statement will be made of what the Corporation undertakes to do with the moneys entrusted to it, and this will at first embrace little more than those things which experience has proved municipalities can perform better than individuals. Tenants, too, will, it is obvious, be far more ready to offer adequate 'rate-rents' if they are given distinctly to understand to what purpose those 'rate-rents' are to be devoted, and after those things are done, and done well, little difficulty will be placed in the way of further appropriate extensions of the field of municipal enterprise.

Our answer, then, to the question, what field is to be covered by municipal enterprise, is this. Its extent will be measured simply by the willingness of the tenants to pay rate-rents, and will grow in proportion as municipal work is done efficiently and honestly, or decline as it is done dishonestly or inefficiently. If, for example, the tenants find that a very small additional contribution, recently made in the shape of 'rate-rent', has enabled the authorities to provide an excellent supply of water for all purposes, and they are convinced that so good a result at so small a cost would not have been achieved through the agency of any private undertaking working for a profit, they will naturally be willing and even anxious that further hopeful-looking experiments in municipal work should be undertaken. The site of Garden City may, in this respect, be compared with Mr. and Mrs. Boffin's famous apartment, which, the reader of Dickens will remember, was furnished at one end to suit the taste of Mrs. Boffin, who was 'a dab at fashion', while at the other end it was furnished to conform to the notions of solid comfort which so gratified Mr. Boffin, but with the mutual understanding between the parties that if Mr. B. should get by degrees to be 'a high-flyer' at fashion, then Mrs. B.'s carpet would gradually 'come for'arder', whilst if Mrs. B. should become 'less of a dab at fashion', Mrs. B.'s carpet would 'go back'arder'. So, in Garden City, if the inhabitants become greater 'dabs' at co-operation, the municipality will 'come for'-arder'; if they become less 'dabs' at co-operation, the municipality will 'go back'arder'; while the relative number of positions occupied by municipal workers and non-municipal workers at any period will very fairly reflect the skill and integrity of the public administration and the degree of value which is therefore associated with municipal effort.

But the municipality of Garden City, besides setting its face against any attempt to embark upon too large a field of enterprise, will so frame its constitution that the responsibility for each branch of the municipal service will be thrown directly upon the officers of that branch and not be practically lost sight of because loosely thrown upon the larger central body—a plan which makes it difficult for the public to perceive where any leakage or friction may be taking place. The constitution is modelled upon that of a large and well-appointed business, which is divided into various departments, each department being expected to justify its own continued existence—its officers being selected, not so much for their knowledge of the business generally as for their special fitness for the work of their department.

THE BOARD OF MANAGEMENT
consists of:

(1) The Central Council.
(2) The Departments.

THE CENTRAL COUNCIL

In this council (or its nominees) are vested the rights and powers of the community as sole landlord of Garden City. Into its treasury are paid (after provision has been made for landlord's rent and sinking fund) all rate-rents received from its tenants, as well as the profits derived from its various municipal undertakings, and these, we have seen, are amply sufficient to discharge all public burdens without any resort to the expedient of compulsory rates. The powers possessed by the Central Council are, it may be noticed in passing, more ample than those possessed by other municipal bodies,[1] for whilst most of these enjoy only such powers as are expressly conferred on them by Acts of Parliament, the Central Council of Garden City exercises on behalf of the people those wider rights, powers and privileges which are enjoyed by landlords under the common law. The private owner of land can do with his land and with the revenue he derives from it what he pleases so long as he is

[1] This important observation of Howard's should be noted by municipal authorities undertaking developments in or outside their own boundaries, as well as by public corporations or private-enterprise bodies undertaking large-scale community-building. *Ed.*

not a nuisance to his neighbour; while, on the other hand, public bodies which acquire land or obtain power to levy rates by Acts of Parliament, can only use that land or spend those rates for such purposes as are expressly prescribed by those Acts. But Garden City is in a greatly superior position, for, by stepping as a *quasi* public body into the rights of a private landlord, it becomes at once clothed with far larger powers for carrying out the will of the people than are possessed by other local bodies, and thus solves to a large extent the problem of local self-government.

But the Central Council, though possessing these large powers, delegates many of them, for convenience of administration, to its various departments, retaining, however, responsibility for:

(1) The general plan on which the estate is laid out.

(2) The amount of money voted to each of the various spending departments, as schools, roads, parks, etc.

(3) Such measure of oversight and control of the departments as is necessary to preserve a general unity and harmony, but no more.

THE DEPARTMENTS
These are divided into various groups—for example:
- (A) Public Control.
- (B) Engineering.
- (C) Social Purposes.

GROUP A, PUBLIC CONTROL
This group may consist of the following sub-groups:

Finance	Assessment
Law	Inspection

Finance
Into this department are paid, after making provision for landlord's rent and sinking fund, all rate-rents; and out of it the necessary sums for the various departments are voted by the Central Council.

Assessment
This department receives all applications from would-be

tenants, and fixes the rate-rent to be paid—such rate-rents not, however, being fixed arbitrarily by the department, but upon the essential principle adopted by other Assessment Committees —the really determining factor being the rate-rent which an average tenant is found willing to pay.[1]

Law

This department settles the terms and conditions under which leases shall be granted, and the nature of the covenants to be entered into by and with the Central Council.

Inspection

This department carries out such reasonable duties in relation to inspection as the municipality, in its capacity of landlord, may with the tenants of the municipality mutually agree upon.

GROUP B, ENGINEERING

This group may consist of the following departments—some of which would be later creations.

Roads	Parks and open spaces
Subways	Drainage
Sewers	Canals
Tramways	Irrigation
Municipal Railway	Water-supply
Public Buildings (other than schools)	Motive-power and Lighting Messages

GROUP C, SOCIAL AND EDUCATIONAL

This group is also divided into various departments, dealing with:

Education	Libraries
Baths and Wash-houses	
Music	Recreation

Election of Members of Board of Management

Members (who may be men or women) are elected by the rate-renters to serve on one or more departments, and the

[1] This individual is known to Assessment Committees under the name of the 'hypothetical tenant'.

Chairmen and Vice-Chairmen of the departments constitute the Central Council.

Under such a constitution it is believed that the community would have the readiest means of rightly estimating the work of its servants, and, at election times, would have clear and distinct issues brought before it. The candidates would not be expected to specify their views upon a hundred and one questions of municipal policy upon which they had no definite opinions, and which would probably not give rise within their term of office to the necessity for recording their votes, but would simply state their views as to some special question or group of questions, a sound opinion upon which would be of urgent importance to the electors, because immediately connected with the welfare of the town.

Chapter Seven

Semi-Municipal Enterprise—Local Option—
Temperance Reform

In the last chapter we saw that no line could be sharply drawn between municipal and individual enterprise, so that one could definitely say of one or the other, 'Hitherto shalt thou come, but no further'; and this ever-changing character of the problem can be usefully illustrated in our examination of the industrial life of Garden City by reference to a form of enterprise there carried on which is neither distinctly municipal nor distinctly individualistic, but partaking, as it does, of the character of both, may be termed 'semi-municipal'.

Among the most reliable sources of revenue possessed by many of our existing municipalities are their so-called 'public markets'. But it is important to notice that these markets are by no means public in the same full sense as are our public parks, libraries, water undertakings, or those numerous other branches of municipal work which are carried on upon public property, by public officials, at the public expense, and solely with a view to the public advantage. On the contrary, our so-called 'public markets' are, for the most part, carried on by private individuals, who pay tolls for the parts of the buildings which they occupy, but who are not, except on a few points, controlled by the municipality, and whose profits are personally enjoyed by the various dealers. Markets may, therefore, be fitly termed *semi-municipal* enterprises.

It would, however, have been scarcely necessary to touch on this question, but that it naturally leads up to the consideration of a form of semi-municipal enterprise which is one of the characteristic features of Garden City. This is to be found in the Crystal Palace, which, it will be remembered, is a wide arcade, skirting the Central Park, in which the most attractive wares on sale in Garden City are exhibited, and, this being a winter garden as well as the great shopping centre, is one of the most

96

favourite resorts of the townspeople. The business at the shops is carried on, not by the municipality, but by various individuals and societies, the number of traders being, however, limited by the principle of local option.

The considerations which have led to this system arise out of the distinction between the cases on the one hand of the manufacturers, and on the other of the distributive societies and shopkeepers who are invited to the town. Thus, for example, in the case of the manufacturer, say, of boots, though he may be glad of the custom of the people of the town, he is by no means dependent on it; his products go all over the world; and he would scarcely wish that the number of boot manufacturers within the area should be specially limited. He would, in fact, lose more than he would gain by restrictions of this kind. A manufacturer frequently prefers to have others carrying on the same trade in his vicinity; for this gives him a larger choice of skilled workmen or workwomen, who themselves desire it also, because it gives them a larger range of employers.

But in the case of shops and stores the case is entirely different. An individual or a society proposing to open in Garden City, say a drapery store, would be most anxious to know what, if any, arrangements were to be made for limiting the number of his competitors, for he would depend almost entirely on the trade of the town or neighbourhood. Indeed it frequently happens that a private landlord, when laying out a building estate, makes arrangements with his shopkeeping tenants designed to prevent them from being swamped by others in the same trade starting on his estate.[1]

The problem, therefore, seems to be how to make such suitable arrangements as will at once:

(1) Induce tenants of the shopkeeping class to come and start in business, offering to the community adequate rate-rents.

[1] Howard's proposals for limiting the number of retail traders, and the class of trade to be carried on in each shop, were adopted at Welwyn Garden City by the Estate Company, though not under the direct democratic control he envisaged. The policy has been the subject of some local controversy, but the results, both on the finance of development and on the quality of retail service given, deserve study. *Ed*.

(2) Prevent the absurd and wasteful multiplication of shops referred to in the note at the foot of page 99.

(3) Secure the advantages usually gained (or supposed to be) by competition—such as low prices, wide range of choice, fair dealing, civility, etc.

(4) Avoid the evils attending monopoly.

All these results may be secured by a simple expedient, which will have the effect of converting competition from an active into a latent force to be brought into play or held in reserve. It is, as we have said, an application of the principle of local option. To explain: Garden City is the sole landlord, and it can grant to a proposed tenant—we will suppose a co-operative society or an individual trader in drapery or fancy goods—a long lease of a certain amount of space in the Grand Arcade (Crystal Palace), at a certain annual rate-rent; and it can say, in effect, to its tenant, 'That site is the only space in that ward which we for the present intend to let to any tenant engaged in your trade. The Arcade is, however, designed to be not only the great shopping centre of the town and district, and the permanent exhibition in which the manufacturers of the town display their wares, but a summer and winter garden. The space this Arcade covers will, therefore, be considerably greater than is actually required for the purposes of shops or stores, if these are kept within reasonable limits. Now, so long as you give satisfaction to the people of the town, none of the space devoted to these recreative purposes will be let to anyone engaged in your calling. It is necessary, however, to guard against monopoly. If, therefore, the people become dissatisfied with your methods of trading, and desire that the force of competition shall be actively brought into play against you, then, on the requisition of a certain number, the necessary space in the Arcade will be allotted by the municipality to some one desirous of starting an opposition store.'

Under this arrangement it will be seen the trader will depend upon the good-will of his customers. If he charges prices which are too high; if he misrepresents the quality of his goods; if he does not treat his employees with proper consideration in regard to hours of labour, wages, or other matters, he will run a great risk of losing the good-will of his customers, and the people of the town will have a method of expressing their sentiments regarding him which will be extremely powerful; they will simply invite a new competitor to enter the field. But, on the other hand, as long as he perform his functions wisely and well, his good-will resting on the solid basis of the good-will of his customers, he will be protected. His advantages are, therefore, enormous. In other towns a competitor might enter the field against him at any moment without warning, perhaps at the very time when he had purchased some expensive goods, which, unless sold during the season, could only be realized at an enormous sacrifice. In Garden City, on the other hand, he has full notice of his danger—time to prepare for it and even to avert it. Besides, the members of the community, except for the purpose of bringing a trader to reason, will not only have no interest in bringing a competitor into the field, but their interests will be best served by keeping competition in the background as long as possible. If the fire of competition is brought to bear upon a trader, they must suffer with him. They will lose space they would far rather see devoted to some other purpose—they will be bound to pay higher prices than those at which the first trader could supply them if he would, and they will have to render municipal services to two traders instead of to one, while the two competitors could not afford to pay so large a sum in rate-rent as could the original trader. For in many cases the effect of competition is to make a rise in price absolutely necessary. Thus, A. has a trade of 100 gallons of milk a day, and can, we will suppose, pay his expenses, earn a bare living, and supply his customers with milk, say, at 4d. a quart. But if a competitor enters the field, then A. can only sell *milk and water* at 4d. a quart if he is to continue to pay his way. Thus the competition of shopkeepers absolutely tends not only to ruin the competitors, but to maintain and even to raise prices, and so to lower real wages.[1]

[1] 'It has been calculated by Mr. Neale' (*Economics of Co-operation*) 'that there are 41,735 separate establishments for twenty-two of the principal retail trades in London. If for each of these trades there were 648 shops—that is nine to the square mile, no one would have to go more than a quarter of a mile to the nearest shop. There would be 14,256 shops in all. Assuming that this supply would be sufficient,

Under this system of local option it will be seen that the tradesmen of the town—be they co-operative societies or individuals—would become, if not strictly or technically so, yet in a very real sense, municipal servants. But they would not be bound up in the red-tape of officialism, and would have the fullest rights and powers of initiation. It would not be by any literal conformity to cast-iron and inflexible rules, but by their skill and judgment in forecasting the wishes and in anticipating the tastes of their constituents, as well as by their integrity and courtesy as business men and women, that they would win and maintain their good-will. They would run certain risks, as all tradesmen must, and in return they would be paid, not of course in the form of salary, but in profits. But the risks they would run would be far less than they must be where competition is unchecked and uncontrolled, while their annual profits in proportion to capital invested might also be greater. They might even sell considerably below the ordinary rate prevailing elsewhere, but yet, having an assured trade and being able very accurately to gauge demand, they might turn their money over with remarkable frequency. Their working expenses, too, would be absurdly small. They would not have to advertise for customers, though they would doubtless make announcements to them of any novelties; but all that waste of effort and of money which is so frequently expended by tradesmen in order to secure customers or to prevent their going elsewhere, would be quite unnecessary.

And not only would each trader be in a sense a municipal servant, but those in his employ would be also. It is true such a trader would have the fullest right to engage and dismiss his servants; but if he acted arbitrarily or harshly, if he paid insufficient wages, or treated his employees inconsiderately, he would certainly run the risk of losing the good-will of the majority of his customers, even although in other respects he might prove himself an admirable public servant. On the other

there are in London 251 shops for every hundred that are really wanted. The general prosperity of the country will be much increased when the capital and labour that are now wastefully employed in the retail trade are set free for other work.' A. and M. P. Marshall, *Economics of Industry*, Chap. IX, sec. 10.

hand, if the example were set of profit-sharing, this might grow into a custom, and the distinction between master and servant would be gradually lost in the simple process of all becoming co-operators.[1]

This system of local option as applied to shopkeeping is not only business-like, but it affords an opportunity for the expression of that public conscience against the sweater which is now being stirred, but which scarcely knows how to effectually respond to the new impulse. Thus there was established in London some years ago the Consumers' League, the object of which was not, as its name might lead one to suspect, to protect the consuming public against the unscrupulous producer, but it was to protect the sweated, over-driven producer against a consuming public over-clamorous for cheapness. Its aim was to assist such of the public as hate and detest the sweating system to avail themselves of the League's carefully compiled information, so that they might be able to studiously avoid the products which had passed through sweaters' hands. But such a movement as the Consumers' League advocated could make but little headway without the support of the shopkeeper. That consumer must be an uncommonly earnest opponent of sweating who insists upon knowing the source whence every article he purchases has come, and a shopkeeper under ordinary circumstances would scarcely be disposed either to give such information or to guarantee that the goods he sold were produced under 'fair' conditions; while to establish shops in large cities, which are already overcrowded with distributive agencies, and to do this with the special object of putting down sweating, is to court

---

[1] This principle of local option, which is chiefly applicable to distributive callings, is perhaps applicable to production in some of its branches. Thus bakeries and laundries, which would largely depend upon the trade of the locality, seem to present instances where it might with some caution be applied. Few businesses seem to require more thorough supervision and control than these, and few have a more direct relation to health. Indeed, a very strong case might be made out for municipal bakeries and municipal laundries, and it is evident that the control of an industry by the community is a half-way house to its assumption of it, should this prove desirable and practicable.

failure. Here in Garden City, however, there will be a splendid opportunity for the public conscience to express itself in this regard, and no shopkeeper will, I hope, venture to sell 'sweated goods'.

There is another question with which the term 'local option' is most closely associated which may be dealt with here. I refer to the temperance question. Now it will be noticed that the municipality, in its position of sole landlord, has the *power* of dealing in the most drastic manner possible with the liquor traffic. There are, as is well known, many landlords who will not permit a public-house to be opened on their estate, and the landlord of Garden City—the people themselves—*could* adopt this course. But would this be wise? I think not. First, such a restriction would keep away the very large and increasing class of moderate drinkers, and would also keep away many of those who are scarcely moderate in their use of alcohol, but as to whom reformers would be most anxious that they should be brought under the healthful influences which would surround them in Garden City. The public-house, or its equivalent, would, in such a community, have many competitors for the favour of the people; while, in large cities, with few opportunities of cheap and rational enjoyment, it has its own way. The experiment, as one in the direction of temperance reform, would, therefore, be more valuable if the traffic were permitted under reasonable regulations than if it were stopped; because, while, in the former case, the effects in the direction of temperance would be clearly traceable to the more natural and healthy form of life, if the latter course were adopted it could only prove, what no one now denies, that it may be possible, by restrictive measures, to entirely keep away the traffic from one small area while intensifying the evils elsewhere.[1]

---

[1] When Howard wrote, there was a strong movement for local option, that is, power of local prohibition of licensed premises by popular vote, and a law to this effect was later enacted for Scotland. In the U.S.A. the movement succeeded in obtaining, for a period, national prohibition. At Letchworth the Estate Company, varying Howard's proposals in this respect, adopted the principle of referring the question of licences to a poll of the adult citizens, who voted against a licence, and to this day continue to do so. No new licensed

But the community would certainly take care to prevent the undue multiplication of licensed houses, and it would be free to adopt any one of the various methods which the more moderate of temperance reformers suggest. The municipal authorities might conduct the liquor traffic themselves, and employ the profits in relief of rates. There is, however, much force in the objection that it is not desirable that the revenue of a community should be so derived, and, therefore, it might be better that the profits should be entirely applied to purposes which would compete with the traffic, or in minimizing its evil effects by establishing asylums for those affected with alcoholism.[1] On this subject, as on all points involved, I earnestly invite correspondence from those who have practical suggestions to offer; and, although the town is but a small one, it would perhaps not be impracticable to test various promising suggestions in the different wards.

public-houses have therefore been built there, though there are several old ones on the estate. At Welwyn Garden City Howard's policy of limiting the number of public-houses, and of regulating their character, was adopted. Ed.

[1] Since To-morrow was published, various companies have been formed with the object of carrying on the trade on principles advocated by the Bishop of Chester. A limited dividend is fixed; all profits beyond are expended in useful public enterprises, and the Managers have no interest whatever in pushing the trade in intoxicating liquors. It may be interesting also to observe that Mr. George Cadbury, in the Deed of Foundation of the Bournville Trust, provided for the complete restriction of the traffic at the outset. But as a practical man he saw that as the Trust grows (and its power of growth is among its most admirable features) it may be necessary to remove such complete restrictions. And he provided that in that event 'all the net profits arising from the sale and co-operative distribution of intoxicating liquors shall be devoted to securing recreation and counter attractions to the liquor trade as ordinarily conducted'. (Note to 1902 edition. Ed.)

Chapter Eight

Pro-Municipal Work

There will be found in every progressive community societies and organizations which represent a far higher level of public spirit and enterprise than that possessed or displayed by such communities in their collective capacity. It is probable that the government of a community can never reach a higher tone or work on a higher plane than the average sense of that community demands and enforces; and it will greatly conduce to the well-being of any society if the efforts of its State or municipal organizations are inspired and quickened by those of its members whose ideals of society duty rise higher than the average.[1]

And so it may be in Garden City. There will be discovered many opportunities for public service which neither the community as a whole, nor even a majority of its members, will at first recognize the importance of, or see their way to embrace, and which public services it would be useless, therefore, to expect the municipality to undertake; but those who have the welfare of society at heart will, in the free air of the city, be always able to experiment on their own responsibility, and thus quicken the public conscience and enlarge the public understanding.

The whole of the experiment which this book describes is indeed of this character. It represents pioneer work, which will

[1] 'Only a proportion of each in one society can have nerve enough to grasp the banner of a new truth, and endurance enough to bear it along rugged and untrodden ways. . . . To insist on a whole community being made at once to submit to the reign of new practices and new ideas which have just begun to commend themselves to the most advanced speculative intelligence of the time—this, even if it were a possible process, would do much to make life impracticable and to hurry on social dissolution. . . . A new social state can never establish its ideas unless the persons who hold them confess them openly and give them an honest and effective adherence.' Mr. John Morley, *On Compromise*, Chap. v.

104

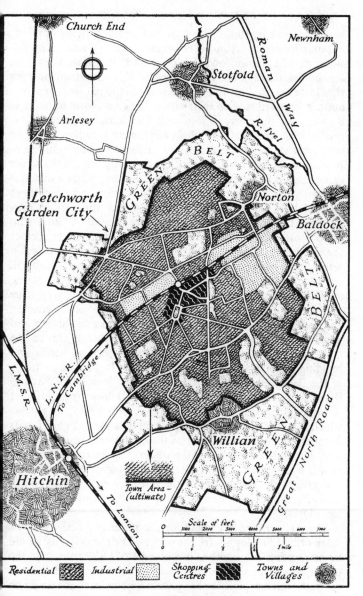

PLAN OF LETCHWORTH

be carried out by those who have not a merely pious opinion, but an effective belief in the economic, sanitary, and social advantages of common ownership of land, and who, therefore, are not satisfied merely to advocate that those advantages should be secured on the largest scale at the national expense, but are impelled to give their views shape and form as soon as they can see their way to join with a sufficient number of kindred spirits. And what the whole experiment is to the nation, so may what we term 'pro-municipal' undertakings be to the community of Garden City or to society generally. Just as the larger experiment is designed to lead the nation into a juster and better system of land tenure and a better and more common-sense view of how towns should be built, so are the various pro-municipal undertakings of Garden City devised by those who are prepared to lead the way in enterprises designed to further the well-being of the town, but who have not as yet succeeded in getting their plans or schemes adopted by the Central Council.

Philanthropic and charitable institutions, religious societies, and educational agencies of various kinds occupy a very large part in this group of pro-municipal or pro-national agencies, and these have been already referred to, and their nature and purposes are well known. But institutions which aim at the more strictly material side of well-being, such as banks and building societies, may be found here too. Just as the founders of the Penny Bank paved the way for the Post Office Savings Bank, so may some of those who study carefully the experiment of building up Garden City see how useful a bank might be, which, like the Penny Bank, aims not so much at gain for its founders as at the well-being of the community at large. Such a bank might arrange to pay the whole of its net profits or all its profits over a certain fixed rate, into the municipal exchequer, and give to the authorities of the town the option of taking it over should they be convinced of its utility and its general soundness.

There is another large field for pro-municipal activity in the work of building homes for the people. The municipality would be attempting too much if it essayed this task, at least at the outset. To do so would be perhaps to depart too widely from the path which experience has justified, however much might be

106

said in favour of such a course on the part of a municipal body in command of ample funds. The municipality has, however, done much to make the building of bright and beautiful homes for the people possible. It has effectually provided against any overcrowding within its area, thus solving a problem found insoluble in existing cities, and it offers sites of ample size at an average rate of £6 per annum for ground rent and rates. Having done so much, the municipality will pay heed to the warning of an experienced municipal reformer, whose desire for the extension of municipal enterprise cannot be doubted (Mr. John Burns, M.P., L.C.C.), who has said: 'A lot of work has been thrown upon the Works Committee of the London County Council by councillors who are so anxious for its success that they would choke it by a burden of work.'

There are, however, other sources to which the workers may look for means to build their own homes. They may form building societies or induce co-operative societies, friendly societies, and trade unions to lend them the necessary money, and to help them to organize the requisite machinery. Granted the existence of the true social spirit, and not its mere letter and name, and that spirit will manifest itself in an infinite variety of ways. There are in this country—who can doubt it?—many individuals and societies who would be ready to raise funds and organize associations for assisting bodies of workmen secure of good wages to build their own homes on favourable terms.

A better security the lenders could scarcely have, especially having regard to the ridiculously small landlord's rent paid by the borrowers. Certain it is that if the building of the homes for these workmen is left to speculative builders of a strongly pronounced individualistic type, and these reap golden harvests, it will be the fault, amongst others, of those large organizations of working men which now place their capital in banks, whence it is withdrawn by those who with it 'exploit' the very men who have placed it there. It is idle for working men to complain of this self-imposed exploitation, and to talk of nationalizing the entire land and capital of this country under an executive of their own class, until they have first been through an apprenticeship at the humbler task of organizing men and women with their own capital in constructive work of a less ambitious character—until they have assisted far more largely than they have yet done in building up capital, not to be wasted in strikes, or employed by capitalists in fighting strikers, but in securing homes and employment for themselves and others on just and honourable terms. The true remedy for capitalist oppression where it exists, is not the strike of *no work*, but the strike of *true work*, and against this last blow the oppressor has no weapon. If labour leaders spent half the energy in co-operative organization that they now waste in co-operative disorganization, the end of our present unjust system would be at hand. In Garden City such leaders will have a fair field for the exercise of pro-municipal functions—functions which are exercised for the municipality, though not by it—and the formation of building societies of this type would be of the greatest possible utility.

But would not the amount of capital required for the building of the dwelling-houses of a town of 30,000 be enormous? Some persons with whom I have discussed the question look at the matter thus. So many houses in Garden City at so many hundred of pounds apiece, capital required so much.[1] This is, of course, quite a mistaken way of regarding the problem. Let us test the matter thus. How many houses have been built in London within the last ten years? Shall we say, at the very roughest of guesses 150,000, costing on an average £300 apiece—to say nothing of shops, factories, and warehouses. Well, that is £45,000,000. Was £45,000,000 raised for this purpose? Yes, certainly, or the houses would not have been built. But the money was not raised all at once, and if one could recognize the actual sovereigns that were raised for the building of these 150,000 houses, one would often find the very same coins turning up again and again. So in Garden City. Before it is completed, there will be 5,500 houses at, say, £300 apiece, making £1,650,000. But this capital will not be raised all at once, and here, far more than in London, the very same sovereigns would be employed in building many houses. For observe, money is not lost or consumed when it is spent. It merely changes hands. A workman of Garden City borrows £200 from a pro-municipal building society, and builds a house with it. That house costs

[1] The position was so stated by Mr. Buckingham in *National Evils and Practical Remedies*, see Chap. x.

him £200, and the 200 sovereigns disappear so far as he is concerned, but they become the property of the brickmakers,
builders, carpenters, plumbers, plasterers, etc., who have built
his house, whence those sovereigns would find their way into
the pockets of the tradesmen and others with whom such workmen deal, and thence would pass into the pro-municipal bank
of the town, when presently, those 200 identical sovereigns
might be drawn out and employed in building another house.
Thus there would be presented the apparent anomaly of two,
and then three, and then four or more houses, each costing
£200, being built with 200 sovereigns.[1] But there is no real
anomaly about it. The coins, of course, did not build the houses
in any of the supposed cases. The coins were but the measure
of value, and like a pair of scales and weights, may be used over
and over again without any perceptible lessening of their worth.
What built the houses was really labour, skill, enterprise, working up the free gifts of nature; and though each of the workers
might have his reward weighed out to him in coins, the cost of
all buildings and works in Garden City must be mainly determined by the skill and energy with which its labours are directed.
Still, so long as gold and silver are recognized as the medium of
exchange, it will be necessary to use them, and of great importance to use them skilfully—for the skill with which they are
used, or their unnecessary use dispensed with, as in a banker's
clearing-house, will have a most important bearing upon the
cost of the town, and upon the annual tax levied in the shape
of interest on borrowed capital. Skill must be therefore directed
to the object of so using coins that they may quickly effect their
object of measuring one value, and be set to work to measure
another—that they may be turned over as many times as possible in the year, in order that the amount of labour measured by
each coin may be as large as possible, and thus the amount
represented by interest on the coins borrowed, though paid at
the normal or usual rate, shall bear as small a proportion as
possible to the amount paid to labour. If this is done effectively,
then a saving to the community in respect of interest as great

---

[1] A similar line of argument to this is very fully elaborated in a
most able work entitled *The Physiology of Industry*, by Mummery
and Hobson (Macmillan & Co.).

as the more easily demonstrated saving in landlord's rent may probably be effected.

And now the reader is asked to observe how admirably, and, as it were, automatically, a well-organized migratory movement to land held in common lends itself to the economic use of money, and to the making of one coin serve many purposes. Money, it is often said, is 'a drug in the market'. Like labour itself, it seems enchanted, and thus one sees millions in gold and silver lying idle in banks facing the very streets where men are wandering workless and penniless. But here, on the site of Garden City, the cry for employment on the part of those willing to work will no more be heard in vain. Only yesterday it may have been so, but to-day the enchanted land is awake, and is loudly calling for its children.[1] There is no difficulty in finding

[1] Mr. A. J. Balfour, M.P., on migration into the towns: 'There could be no doubt that when there was agricultural distress, migration into the towns must increase, but do not let any Member suppose that if agriculture were as prosperous now as it was twenty years ago, or as the dreams of the greatest dreamers of dreams would make it, you could by any possibility stop this immigration from the country. It depends upon causes and natural laws which no laws we can pass can permanently modify. The plain fact is, that in a rural district there is and can be only one investment for capital, and only one employment for labour. When prosperity in agriculture increases, immigration into towns diminishes, no doubt: but however prosperous agriculture may be, a normal point must be reached when no more capital can be applied to the land, and no more labour can be applied, and when you have reached that point it does, of necessity, happen that if marriages occur with the frequency with which they occur at the present time, and if families are as large as they are at the present time, there must be an immigration from the country to the town, from the place where there is only one kind of employment of labour, strictly limited by the natural capacity of the soil, to another place where there is no limit whatever to the employment of labour, except the limit set by the amount of capital seeking investment, and the amount of labour capable of taking advantage of that capital. If that were an abstruse doctrine of political economy, I should be afraid to mention it in this House, where political economy has become a bye-word and reproach. But it is really a plain statement of a natural law which I most earnestly advise every man to take to heart.' *Parliamentary Debates*, 12th December 1893.

work—profitable work—work that is really urgently, imperatively needed—the building of a home-city, and, as men hasten to build up this and the other towns which must inevitably follow its construction, the migration to the towns—the old, crowded, chaotic slum towns of the past—will be effectually checked, and the current of population set in precisely the opposite direction—to the new towns, bright and fair, wholesome and beautiful.

Chapter Nine

Some Difficulties Considered

'Watt was often consulted about supposed inventions and discoveries, and his invariable reply was to recommend that a model should be formed and tried. This he considered as the only true test of the value of any novelty in mechanics.'—*Book of Days*.

'Selfish and contentious men will not cohere, and without coherence nothing can be accomplished.'—CHARLES DARWIN, *Descent of Man* (1871).

'The difficulty felt about Communism, or even about any fairly complete Socialism, is that it interferes with man's freedom to make demands for his many-sided nature, and to endeavour to satisfy those demands. It secures bread to all, perhaps, but it ignores the doctrine that man shall not live by bread alone. The future probably lies with those who, instead of pitting against one another, Socialism and Individualism, will seek to realize a true, vital, organic conception of Society and of the State in which both Individualism and Socialism will have their proper share. The bark which carries civilized man with his fortunes will thus steer an even course between the Scylla of anarchy and the Charybdis of despotism.'—*Daily Chronicle*, 2nd July 1894.

Having now, in a concrete rather than an abstract form, stated the objects and purposes of our scheme, it may be well to deal, though somewhat briefly, with an objection which may arise in the thought of the reader: 'Your scheme may be very attractive, but it is but one of a great number, many of which have been tried and have met with but little success. How do you distinguish it from those? How, in the face of such a record of failure, do you expect to secure that large measure of public support which is necessary ere such a scheme can be put into operation?'

The question is a very natural one, and demands an answer. My reply is: It is quite true that the pathway of experiment towards a better state of society is strewn with failures. But so is the pathway of experiment to any result that is worth achieving. Success is, for the most part, built on failure. As Mrs. Humphry Ward remarks in *Robert Elsmere*: 'All great changes are preceded by numbers of sporadic, and, as the bystander thinks, intermittent efforts.' A successful invention or discovery is usually a slow growth, to which new elements are added, and from which old elements are removed, first in the thought of the inventor, and subsequently in an outward form, until at last precisely the right elements and no others are brought together. Indeed, it may be truly said that if you find a series of experiments continued through many years by various workers, there will eventually be produced the result for which so many have been industriously searching. Long-continued effort, in spite of failure and defeat, is the forerunner of complete success. He who wishes to achieve success may turn past defeat into future victory by observing one condition. He must profit by past experiences, and aim at retaining all the strong points without the weaknesses of former efforts.

To deal at all exhaustively here with the history of social experiments would be beyond the scope of this book; but a few leading features may be noticed with a view to meeting the objection with which this chapter opens.

Probably the chief cause of failure in former social experiments has been a misconception of the principal element in the problem—human nature itself. The degree of strain which average human nature will bear in an altruistic direction has not been duly considered by those who have essayed the task of suggesting new forms of social organization. A kindred mistake has arisen from regarding one principle of action to the exclusion of others. Take Communism, for instance. Communism is a most excellent principle, and all of us are Communists in some degree, even those who would shudder at being told so. For we all believe in communistic roads, communistic parks, and communistic libraries. But though Communism is an excellent principle, Individualism is no less excellent. A great orchestra which enraptures us with its delightful music is composed of men and women who are accustomed not only to play together, but to practise separately, and to delight themselves and their friends by their own, it may be comparatively, feeble efforts. Nay, more: isolated and individual thought and action are as essential, if the best results of combination are to be secured, as combination and co-operation are essential, if the best results of isolated effort are to be gained. It is by isolated thought that new combinations are worked out; it is through the lessons learned in associated effort that the best individual work is accomplished; and that society will prove the most healthy and vigorous where the freest and fullest opportunities are afforded alike for individual and for combined effort.

Now, do not the whole series of communistic experiments owe their failure largely to this—that they have not recognized this duality of principle, but have carried one principle, excellent enough in itself, altogether too far? They have assumed that because common property is good, all property should be common; that because associated effort can produce marvels, individual effort is to be regarded as dangerous, or at least futile, some extremists even seeking to abolish altogether the idea of the family or home. No reader will confuse the experiment here advocated with any experiment in absolute Communism.

Nor is the scheme to be regarded as a socialistic experiment. Socialists, who may be regarded as Communists of a more moderate type, advocate common property in land and in all the instruments of production, distribution, and exchange—railways, machinery, factories, docks, banks, and the like; but they would preserve the principle of private ownership in all such things as have passed in the form of wages to the servants of the community, with the proviso, however, that these wages shall not be employed in organized creative effort, involving the employment of more than one person; for all forms of employment with a view to remuneration should, as the Socialists contend, be under the direction of some recognized department of the Government, which is to claim a rigid monopoly. But it is very doubtful whether this principle of the Socialist, in which there is a certain measure of recognition of the individual side of man's nature as well as of his social side, represents a basis on which an experiment can fairly proceed with the hope of permanent success. Two chief difficulties appear to present themselves. First, the self-seeking side of man—his too frequent desire to produce, with a view to possessing for his own personal use and enjoyment; and, secondly, his love of independence and of initiative, his personal ambition, and his consequent unwillingness to put himself under the guidance of others for the whole of his working day, with little opportunity of striking out some independent line of action, or of taking a leading part in the creation of new forms of enterprise.

Now, even if we pass over the first difficulty—that of human self-seeking—even if we assume that we have a body of men and women who have realized the truth that concerted social effort will achieve far better results in enjoyable commodities for each member of the community than can possibly be achieved by ordinary competitive methods—each struggling for himself—we have still the other difficulty, arising out of the higher and not the lower nature of the men and women who are to be organized—their love of independence and of initiative. Men love combined effort, but they love individual effort, too, and they will not be content with such few opportunities for personal effort as they would be allowed to make in a rigid socialistic community. Men do not object to being organized under competent leadership, but some also want to be leaders, and to have a share in the work of organizing; they like to lead as well as to be led. Besides, one can easily imagine men filled with a desire to serve the community in some way which the community as a whole did not at the moment appreciate the advantage of, and who would be precluded by the very constitution of the socialistic state from carrying their proposals into effect.

Now, it is at this very point that a most interesting experiment at Topolobampo has broken down. The experiment, which was initiated by Mr. A. K. Owen, an American civil engineer, was started on a considerable tract of land obtained under concession from the Mexican Government. One principle adopted by Mr. Owen was that 'all employment must be through the Department for the Diversity of Home Industries. One member cannot directly employ another member, and only members can be employed through the settlement.'[1] In other words, if A. and B. were dissatisfied with the management,

[1] A. K. Owen, *Integral Co-operation at Work* (U.S. Book Co., 150 Worth St., N.Y., 1885).

whether owing to doubts as to its competency or honesty, they could not arrange to work with each other, even though their sole desire might be the common good; but they must leave the settlement. And this is what they accordingly did in very considerable numbers.

It is at this point that a great distinction between the Topolobampo experiment and the scheme advocated in this work is evident. In Topolobampo the organization claimed a monopoly of all productive work, and each member must work under the direction of those who controlled that monopoly, or must leave the organization. In Garden City no such monopoly is claimed, and any dissatisfaction with the public administration of the affairs of the town would no more necessarily lead to a widespread split in Garden City than in any other municipality. At the outset, at least, by far the larger part of the work done will be by individuals or combinations of individuals quite other than municipal servants, just as in any other municipality, at present existing, the sphere of municipal work is still very small as compared with the work performed by other groups.

Other sources of failure in some social experiments are the considerable expense incurred by migrants before they reach the scene of their future labours, the great distance from any large market, and the difficulty of previously obtaining any real knowledge of the conditions of life and labour there prevailing. The one advantage gained—cheap land—seems to be altogether insufficient to compensate for these and other disadvantages.

We now come to what is perhaps the chief difference between the scheme advocated in this work and most other schemes of a like nature which have been hitherto advocated or put into actual practice. That difference is this: While others have sought to weld into one large organization individuals who have not yet been combined into smaller groups, or who must leave those smaller groups on their joining the larger organization, my proposal appeals not only to individuals but to co-operators, manufacturers, philanthropic societies, and others experienced in organization, and with organizations under their control, to come and place themselves under conditions involving no new restraints but rather securing wider freedom. And, further, a striking feature of the present scheme is that the very considerable number of persons already engaged on the estate will not be displaced (except those on the town site, and these gradually), but these will themselves form a valuable nucleus, paying in rents, from the very inception of the enterprise, a sum which will go very far towards the interest on the money with which the estate is purchased—rents which they will be more willing to pay to a landlord who will treat them with perfect equity, and who will bring to their doors consumers for their produce. The work of organization is, therefore, in a very large measure accomplished. The army is now in existence; it has but to be mobilized; it is with no undisciplined mob that we have to deal. Or the comparison between this experiment and those which have preceded it is like that between two machines—one of which has to be created out of various ores which have first to be gathered together and then cast into various shapes, while for the other all the parts are ready to hand and have but to be fitted together.

Chapter Ten

A Unique Combination of Proposals

'Human beings, in their present condition, may be likened to bees in the act of swarming, as we see them clinging in a mass to a single bough. Their position is a temporary one, and must inevitably be changed. They must rise and find themselves a new abode. Every bee knows this, and is eager to shift its own position, as well as that of the others, but not one of them will do so until the whole swarm rises. The swarm cannot rise, because one bee clings to the other and prevents it from separating itself from the swarm, and so they all continue to hang. It might seem as if there were no deliverance from this position, precisely as it seems to men of the world who have become entangled in the social net. Indeed, there would be no outlet for the bees if each one were not a living creature possessed of a pair of wings. Neither would there be any issue for men if each one were not a living individual being, gifted with a capacity for assimilating the Christian life-conception. If among these bees who are able to fly not one could be found willing to start, the swarm would never change its position. And it is the same among men. If the man who has assimilated the Christian life-conception waits for others before he proceeds to live in accordance with it, mankind will never change its attitude. And as all that is needed to change a solid mass of bees into a flying swarm is for one bee to spread its wings and fly away, when the second, the third, the tenth and the hundredth will follow suit; so all that is needed to break through the magic circle of social life, deliverance from which seems so hopeless, is that one man should view life from a Christian standpoint and begin to frame his own life accordingly, whereupon others will follow in his footsteps.'
—LEO TOLSTOY, *The Kingdom of God is Within You* (1893).

In the last chapter, I pointed out the great differences of principle between the project placed before the reader of this work and some of those schemes of social reform which, having been put to the test of experience, have ended in disaster, and I urged that there were features of the proposed experiment which so completely distinguished it from those unsuccessful schemes that they could not be fairly regarded as any indication of the results which would probably follow from launching this experiment.

It is my present purpose to show that though the scheme taken as a whole is a new one, and is, perhaps, entitled to some consideration on that account, its chief claim upon the attention of the public lies in the fact that it combines the important features of several schemes which have been advocated at various times, and so combines them as to secure the best results of each, without the dangers and difficulties which sometimes, even in the minds of their authors, were clearly and distinctly seen.

Shortly stated, my scheme is a combination of three distinct projects which have, I think, never been united before. These are: (1) The proposals for an organized migratory movement of population of Edward Gibbon Wakefield and of Professor Alfred Marshall; (2) the system of land tenure first proposed by Thos. Spence and afterwards (though with an important modification) by Mr. Herbert Spencer; and (3) the model city of James Silk Buckingham.[1]

Let us take these proposals in the order named. Wakefield, in his *Art of Colonization* (J. W. Parker, London, 1849), urged that colonies when formed—he was not thinking of home colonies —should be based on scientific principles. He said (p. 109): 'We send out colonies of the limbs, without the belly and the head, of needy persons, many of them mere paupers, or even criminals; colonies made up of *a single class of persons* in the community, and that the most helpless and the most unfit to perpetuate our national character, and to become the fathers of a race whose habits of thinking and feeling shall correspond to those which, in the meantime, we are cherishing at home. The ancients, on the contrary, sent out *a representation of the parent State—colonists from all ranks*. We stock the farm with creeping

[1] I may, perhaps, state as showing how in the search for truth men's minds run in the same channels, and as, possibly, some additional argument for the soundness of the proposals thus combined, that, till I had got far on with my project, I had not seen either the proposals of Professor Marshall or of Wakefield (beyond a very short reference to the latter in J. S. Mill's *Elements of Political Economy*), nor had I seen the work of Buckingham, which, published nearly fifty years ago, seems to have attracted but little attention.

and climbing plants, without any trees of firmer growth for them to entwine round. A hop-ground without poles, the plants matted confusedly together, and scrambling on the ground in tangled heaps, with here and there some clinging to rank thistles and hemlock, would be an apt emblem of a modern colony. The ancients began by nominating to the honourable office of captain or leader of the colony one of the chief men, if not the chief man of the State, like the queen bee leading the workers. Monarchies provided a prince of the royal blood; an aristocracy its choicest nobleman; a democracy its most influential citizen. These naturally carried along with them some of their own station in life—their companions and friends; some of their immediate dependants also—of those between themselves and the lowest class; and were encouraged in various ways to do so. The lowest class again followed with alacrity, because they found themselves moving *with* and not *away from* the state of society in which they had been living. It was the same social and political union under which they had been born and bred; and to prevent any contrary impression being made, the utmost solemnity was observed in transferring the rites of pagan superstition. They carried with them their gods, their festivals, their games—all, in short, that held together and kept entire the fabric of society as it existed in the parent state. Nothing was left behind that could be moved of all that the heart or eye of an exile misses. The new colony was made to appear as if time or chance had reduced the whole community to smaller dimensions, leaving it still essentially the same home and country to its surviving members. It consisted of a general contribution of members from all classes, and so became, on its first settlement, a mature state, with all the component parts of that which sent it forth. It was a transfer of population, therefore, which gave rise to no sense of degradation, as if the colonist were thrust out from a higher to a lower description of community.'[1]

[1] Howard was mistaken in attributing this passage to Wakefield. The latter quotes it in his *Art of Colonization* from an appendix by Dr. Hind (Dean of Carlisle) to *Thoughts on Secondary Punishment* (1832). It is of course consistent with Wakefield's advocacy of the colonization of Australia and New Zealand by balanced groups of migrants. *Ed.*

J. S. Mill, in his *Elements of Political Economy*, Book I, chap. VIII, sec. 3, says of this work: 'Wakefield's theory of colonization has excited much attention, and is doubtless destined to excite much more. . . . His system consists of arrangements for securing that each colony shall have from the first a town population bearing due proportion to the agricultural, and that the cultivators of the soil shall not be so widely scattered as to be deprived by distance of the benefit of that town population as a market for their produce.'

Professor Marshall's proposals for an organized migratory movement of population from London have been already noticed,[1] but the following passage from the article already referred to may be quoted:

'There might be great variety of method, but the general plan would probably be for a committee, whether formed specially for the purpose or not, to interest themselves in the formation of a colony in some place well beyond the range of London smoke. After seeing their way to building or buying suitable cottages there, they would enter into communication with some of the employers of low-waged labour. They would select, at first, industries that used very little fixed capital; and, as we have seen, it fortunately happens that most of the industries which it is important to move are of this kind. They would find an employer—and there must be many such—who really cares for the misery of his employees. Acting with him and by his advice, they would make themselves the friends of people employed or fit to be employed in his trade; they would show them the advantages of moving, and help them to move, both with counsel and money. They would organize the sending of work backwards and forwards, the employer perhaps opening an agency in the colony. But after being once started it ought to be self-supporting, for the cost of carriage, even if the employees went in sometimes to get instructions, would be less than the saving made in rent—at all events, if allowance be made for the value of the garden produce. And more than as much gain would probably be saved by removing the temptation to drink which is caused by the sadness of London. They would meet with much passive resistance at first. The unknown has terrors

[1] Chapter III, page 66.

to all, but especially to those who have lost their natural spring. Those who have lived always in the obscurity of a London court might shrink away from the free light; poor as are their acquaintanceships at home, they might fear to go where they knew no one. But, with gentle insistence, the committee would urge their way, trying to get those who knew one another to move together, by warm, patient sympathy, taking off the chill of the first change. It is only the first step that costs; every succeeding step would be easier. The work of several firms, not always in the same business, might, in some cases, be sent together. Gradually a prosperous industrial district would grow up, and then, mere self-interest would induce employers to bring down their main workshops, and even to start factories in the colony. Ultimately all would gain, but most the landowners and the railroads connected with the colony.'[1]

What could more strongly point than the last sentence of that quotation from Professor Marshall's proposal to the necessity of first *buying* the land, so that the most admirable project of Thomas Spence can be put into practice, and thus prevent the terrible rise in rent which Professor Marshall foresees? Spence's proposal, put forward more than a hundred years ago, at once suggests how to secure the desired end. Here it is:

'Then you may behold the rent which the people have paid into the parish treasuries employed by each parish in paying the Government its share of the sum which the Parliament or National Congress at any time grants; in maintaining and relieving its own poor and people out of work; in paying the necessary officers their salaries; in building, repairing, and adorning its houses, bridges, and other structures; in making and maintaining convenient and delightful streets, highways, and passages, both for foot and carriages; in making and maintaining canals and other conveniences for trade and navigation; in planting and taking in waste grounds; in premiums for the encouragement of agriculture or anything else thought worthy of encouragement; and, in a word, in doing whatever the people

[1] The project of *one* large London manufacturer transferring his works from the east end of London to the country is the chief theme of a story entitled *Nineteen Hundred?*, by Marianne Farningham (London, 1892).

think proper, and not, as formerly, to support and spread luxury, pride, and all manner of vice. . . . There are no tolls or taxes of any kind paid among them by native or foreigner but the aforesaid rent, which every person pays to the parish, according to the quantity, quality, and conveniences of the land . . . he occupies in it. The government, poor, roads, etc. . . . are all maintained with the rent, on which account all wares, manufactures, allowable trade employments or actions are entirely duty free.' (From a lecture read at the Philosophical Society in Newcastle, on 8th November 1775, for printing which the Society did the author the honour to expel him.)

It will be observed that the only difference between this proposal and the proposals as to land reform put forward in this book, is not a difference of system, but a difference (and a very important one) as to the *method* of its inauguration. Spence appears to have thought that the people would, by a fiat, dispossess the existing owners and establish the system at once and universally throughout the country; while, in this work, it is proposed to purchase the necessary land with which to establish the system on a small scale, and to trust to the inherent advantages of the system leading to its gradual adoption.

Writing some seventy years after Spence had put forward his proposal, Mr. Herbert Spencer (having first laid down the grand principle that all men are equally entitled to the use of the earth, as a corollary of the law of equal liberty generally), in discussing this subject, observes, with his usual force and clearness:

'But to what does this doctrine that men are equally entitled to the use of the earth, lead? Must we return to the times of unenclosed wilds, and subsist on roots, berries, and game? Or are we to be left to the management of Messrs. Fourier, Owen, Louis Blanc & Co.? Neither. Such a doctrine is consistent with the highest civilization, may be carried out without involving a community of goods, and need cause no very serious revolution in existing arrangements. The change required would be simply a change of landlords. Separate ownership would merge in the joint-stock ownership of the public. Instead of being in the possession of individuals, the country would be held by the great corporate body—society. Instead of leasing his acres from an isolated proprietor, the farmer would lease them from the nation. Instead of paying his rent to the agent of Sir John and His Grace, he would pay it to an agent or deputy agent of the community. Stewards would be public officials instead of private ones, and tenancy the only land tenure. A state of things so ordered would be in perfect harmony with the moral law. Under it all men would be equally landlords; all men would be alike free to become tenants. A., B., C. and the rest might compete for a vacant farm as now, and one of them might take that farm without in any way violating the principles of pure equity. All would be equally free to bid; all would be equally free to refrain. And when the farm had been let to A., B., or C., all parties would have done that which they willed, the one in choosing to pay a given sum to his fellow men for the use of certain lands—the others in refusing to pay the sum. Clearly, therefore, on such a system the earth might be enclosed, occupied, and cultivated in entire subordination to the law of equal freedom.' (*Social Statics*, Chap. IX, sec. 8.)

But having thus written, Mr. Herbert Spencer at a later period, having discovered two grave difficulties in the way of his own proposal, unreservedly withdrew it. The first of these difficulties was the evils which he considered as inseparable from State ownership (see *Justice*, published in 1891, Appendix B, p. 290); the second, the impossibility, as Mr. Spencer regarded it, of acquiring the land on terms which would be at once equitable to existing owners and remunerative to the community.

But if the reader examines the scheme of Spence, which preceded the now-withdrawn proposals of Mr. Herbert Spencer, he will see that Spence's scheme was entirely freed (as is the one put forward in this little book), from the objections which might probably attend control by the State.[1] The rents were, under Spence's proposals, as in my own, not to be levied by a *Central Government* far removed from contact with the people, but by the very parish (in my scheme the municipality) in which the people reside. As to the other difficulty which presented itself to Mr. Herbert Spencer's mind—that of acquiring the land on

[1] Though Mr. Herbert Spencer, as if to rebuke his own theory that State control is inherently bad, says, 'Political speculation which sets out with the assumption that the State has in all cases the same nature must end in profoundly erroneous conclusions.'

equitable terms, and of yet making it remunerative to the pur-
chasers—a difficulty which Mr. Herbert Spencer, seeing no way
out of, rashly concluded to be insuperable—that difficulty is
entirely removed by my proposal of buying agricultural or
sparsely settled land, letting it in the manner advocated by
Spence, and then bringing about the scientific migratory movement advocated by Wakefield and (though in a somewhat less
daring fashion) by Professor Marshall.

Surely a project, which thus brings what Mr. Herbert Spencer
still terms 'the dictum of absolute ethics'—that all men are
equally entitled to the use of the earth—into the field of practical
life, and makes it a thing immediately realizable by those who
believe in it, must be one of the greatest public importance.
When a great philosopher in effect says, we cannot conform our
life to the highest moral principles because men have laid an
immoral foundation for us in the past, but 'if, while possessing
those ethical sentiments which social discipline has now produced, men stood in possession of a territory not yet individually
portioned out, they would no more hesitate to assert equality of
their claims to the land than they would hesitate to assert
equality of their claims to light and air'[1]—one cannot help
wishing—so inharmonious does life seem—that the opportunity
presented itself of migrating to a new planet where the 'ethical
sentiments which social discipline has now produced' might be
indulged in. But a new planet, or even 'a territory not yet individually portioned out', is by no means necessary if we are but
in real earnest; for it has been shown that an organized, migratory movement from over-developed, high-priced land to comparatively raw and unoccupied land, will enable all who desire
it to live this life of equal freedom and opportunity; and a sense
of the possibility of a life on earth at once orderly and free
dawns upon the heart and mind.

The third proposal which I have combined with those of
Spence and Mr. Herbert Spencer, of Wakefield and Professor
Marshall, embraces one essential feature of a scheme of James
S. Buckingham,[2] though I have purposely omitted some of the

[1] *Justice*, Chap. XI, p. 85.

[2] Buckingham's scheme is set forth in a work entitled *National
Evils and Practical Remedies*, published by Peter Jackson, St. Mar-
tins le Grand, about 1849.

essential features of that scheme. Mr. Buckingham says (p. 25):
'My thoughts were thus directed to the great defects of all existing towns, and the desirability of forming at least one model
town which should avoid the most prominent of these defects,
and substitute advantages not yet possessed by any.' In his work
he exhibits a ground plan and a sketch of a town of about 1,000
acres, containing a population of 25,000, and surrounded by a
large agricultural estate. Buckingham, like Wakefield, saw the
great advantages to be derived by combining an agricultural
community with an industrial, and urged: 'Wherever practicable, the labours of agriculture and manufacture to be so
mingled and the variety of fabrics and materials to be wrought
upon also so assorted as to make short periods of labour on
each alternately with others produce that satisfaction and freedom from tedium and weariness which an unbroken round of
monotonous occupation so frequently occasions, and because
also variety of employment develops the mental as well as
physical faculties much more perfectly than any single occupation.'

But though on these points the scheme is strikingly like my
own, it is also a very different one. Buckingham having traced,
as he thought, the evils of society to their source in competition,
intemperance, and war, proposed to annihilate competition by
forming a system of complete or integral co-operation; to remove intemperance by the total exclusion of intoxicants; to put
an end to war by the absolute prohibition of gunpowder. He
proposed to form a large company, with a capital of £4,000,000;
to buy a large estate, and to erect churches, schools, factories,
warehouses, dining-halls, dwelling-houses, at rents varying from
£30 a year to £300 a year; and to carry on all productive operations, whether agricultural or industrial, as one large undertaking covering the whole field and permitting no rivals.

Now it will be seen that though in outward form Buckingham's scheme and my own present the same feature of a model
town set in a large agricultural estate, so that industrial and
farming pursuits might be carried on in a healthy, natural way,
yet the inner life of the two communities would be entirely
different—the inhabitants of Garden City enjoying the fullest
rights of free association, and exhibiting the most varied forms

of individual and co-operative work and endeavour, the members of Buckingham's city being held together by the bonds of a rigid cast-iron organization, from which there could be no escape but by leaving the association, or breaking it up into various sections.

To sum up this chapter. My proposal is that there should be an earnest attempt made to organize a migratory movement of population from our overcrowded centres to sparsely settled rural districts; that the mind of the public should not be confused, or the efforts of organizers wasted in a premature attempt to accomplish this work on a national scale, but that great thought and attention shall be first concentrated on a single movement yet one sufficiently large to be at once attractive and resourceful; that the migrants shall be guaranteed (by the making of suitable arrangements before the movement commences) that the whole increase in land values due to their migration shall be secured to them; that this be done by creating an organization, which, while permitting its members to do those things which are good in their own eyes (provided they infringe not the rights of others) shall receive all 'rate-rents' and expend them in those public works which the migratory movement renders necessary or expedient—thus eliminating rates, or, at least, greatly reducing the necessity for any compulsory levy; and that the golden opportunity afforded by the fact that the land to be settled upon has but few buildings or works upon it, shall be availed of in the fullest manner, by so laying out a Garden City that, as it grows, the free gifts of Nature—fresh air, sunlight, breathing room and playing room—shall be still retained in all needed abundance, and by so employing the resources of modern science that Art may supplement Nature, and life may become an abiding joy and delight. And it is important to notice that this proposal, so imperfectly put forward, is no scheme hatched in a restless night in the fevered brain of an enthusiast, but is one having its origin in the thoughtful study of many minds, and the patient effort of many earnest souls, each bringing some element of value, till, the time and the opportunity having come, the smallest skill avails to weld those elements into an effective combination.

Chapter Eleven

The Path followed up

'How can a man learn to know himself? By reflection never—only by action. In the measure that thou seekest to do thy duty shalt thou know what is in thee. But what is thy duty? The demand of the hour.'—GOETHE.

The reader is now asked to kindly assume, for the sake of argument, that our Garden City experiment has been fairly launched, and is a decided success, and to consider briefly some of the more important effects which such an object lesson, by the light which it will throw upon the pathway of reform, must inevitably produce upon society, and then we will endeavour to trace some of the broader features of the after-development.

Among the greatest needs of man and of society to-day, as at all times, are these: A worthy aim and opportunity to realize it; work and ends worth working for. All that a man is, and all that he may become, is summed up in his aspirations, and this is no less true of society than of the individual. The end I venture to now set before the people of this country and of other countries is no less 'noble and adequate' than this, that they should forthwith gird themselves to the task of building up clusters of beautiful home-towns, each zoned by gardens, for those who now dwell in crowded, slum-infested cities. We have already seen how *one* such town may be built; let us now see how the true path of reform, once discovered, will, if resolutely followed, lead society on to a far higher destiny than it has ever yet ventured to hope for, though such a future has often been foretold by daring spirits.

There have in the past been inventions and discoveries on the making of which society has suddenly leaped upward to a new and higher plane of existence. The utilization of steam—a force long recognized, but which proved somewhat difficult to harness to the task it was fitted to accomplish—effected mighty changes; but the discovery of a method for giving effect to a far greater

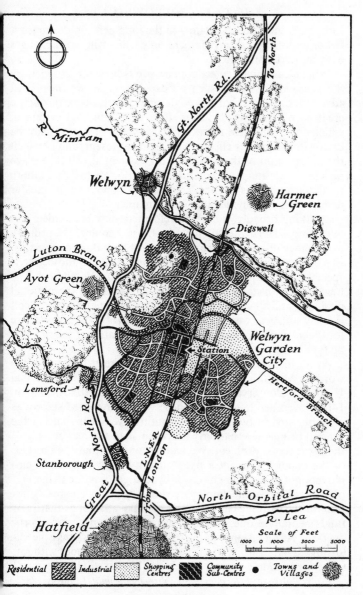

PLAN OF WELWYN

force than the force of steam—to the long pent-up desire for a better and nobler social life here on earth—will work changes even more remarkable.

What clearly marked economic truth is brought into view by the successful issue of such an experiment as we have been advocating? This: That there is a broad path open, through a creation of new wealth forms, to a new industrial system in which the productive forces of society and of nature may be used with far greater effectiveness than at present, and in which the distribution of the wealth forms so created will take place on a far juster and more equitable basis. Society may have more to divide among its members, and at the same time the greater dividend may be divided in a juster manner.

Speaking broadly, industrial reformers may be divided into two camps. The first camp includes those who urge the primary importance of paying close and constant attention to the necessity of *increased production*: the second includes those whose special aim is directed to *more just and equitable division*. The former are constantly saying, in effect, 'Increase the national dividend, and all will be well'; the latter, 'The national dividend is fairly sufficient were it but divided equitably.' The former are for the most part of the individualistic, the latter of the socialistic type.

As an instance of the former point of view, I may cite the words of Mr. A. J. Balfour, who, at a Conference of the National Union of Conservative Associations held at Sunderland on 14th November 1894 said: 'Those who represented society as if it consisted of two sections disputing over their share of the general produce were utterly mistaken as to the real bearing of the great social problem. We had to consider that the produce of the country was not a fixed quantity, of which, if the employers got more, the employed would get less, or if the employed got more, the employers would get less. The real question for the working classes of this country was not primarily or fundamentally a question of division :-it was a question of production.' As an instance of the second point of view, take the following: 'The absurdity of the notion of raising the poor without, to a corresponding degree, depressing the rich will be obvious.'[1]

[1] Frank Fairman, *Principles of Socialism made plain* (London, 1888).

I have already shown, and I hope to make this contention yet more clear, that there is a path along which sooner or later, both the Individualist and the Socialist must inevitably travel; for I have made it abundantly clear that on a small scale society may readily become more individualistic than now—if by Individualism is meant a society in which there is fuller and freer opportunity for its members to do and to produce what they will, and to form free associations, of the most varied kinds; while it may also become more socialistic—if by Socialism is meant a condition of life in which the well-being of the community is safeguarded, and in which the collective spirit is manifested by a wide extension of the area of municipal effort. To achieve these desirable ends, I have taken a leaf out of the books of each type of reformer and bound them together by a thread of practicability. Not content with *urging* the necessity of increased production, I have shown *how it can be achieved*; while the other and equally important end of more equitable distribution is, as I have shown, easily possible, and in a manner which need cause no ill-will, strife, or bitterness; is constitutional; requires no revolutionary legislation; and involves no direct attack upon vested interests. Thus may the desires of the two sections of reformers to whom I have referred be attained. I have, in short, followed out Lord Rosebery's suggestion, and 'borrowed from Socialism its large conception of common effort, and its vigorous conception of municipal life, and from Individualism the preservation of self-respect and self-reliance', and, by a concrete illustration, I have, I think, disproved the cardinal contention of Mr. Benjamin Kidd in his famous book, *Social Evolution*, that 'the interests of the social organism and of the individuals comprising it at any particular time are actually antagonistic; they can never be reconciled; they are inherently and essentially irreconcilable'.

Most socialistic writers appear to me to exhibit too keen a desire to appropriate old forms of wealth, either by purchasing out or by taxing out the owners, and they seem to have little conception that the truer method is to create new forms and to create them under juster conditions. But this latter conception should inevitably follow an adequate realization of the ephemeral nature of most forms of wealth; and there is no truth more fully recognized by economic writers than that nearly all forms of material wealth, except, indeed, the planet on which we live and the elements of nature, are extremely fugitive and prone to decay. Thus for instance, J. S. Mill, in *Elements of Political Economy*, Book 1, Chapter V, says: 'The greater part in value of the wealth now existing in England has been produced by human hands within the last twelve months. A very small proportion indeed of that large aggregate was in existence ten years ago; of the present productive capital of the country, scarcely any part except farmhouses and manufactories and a few ships and machines; and even these would not in most cases have survived so long if fresh labour had not been employed within that period in putting them into repair. The land subsists, and the land is almost the only thing that subsists.' The leaders of the great socialistic movement, of course, know all this perfectly well; yet this quite elementary truth seems to fade from their minds when they are discussing methods of reform, and they appear to be as anxious to seize upon present forms of wealth as if they regarded them as of a really lasting and permanent nature.

But this inconsistency of socialistic writers is all the more striking when one remembers that these writers are the very ones who insist most strongly upon the view that a very large part of the wealth-forms now in existence are not really *wealth* at all—that they are 'ilth', and that any form of society which represents even a step towards their ideal must involve the sweeping away of such forms and the creation of new forms in their place. With a degree of inconsistency that is positively startling, they exhibit an insatiable desire to become possessed of these forms of wealth which are not only rapidly decaying, but are in their opinion absolutely useless or injurious.

Thus Mr. H. M. Hyndman, at a lecture delivered at the Democratic Club, 29th March 1893, said: 'It was desirable that they should map out and formulate socialistic ideas which they should desire to see brought about when the so-called Individualism of the present day has broken down, as it inevitably would do. One of the first things that they as Socialists would have to do would be to depopulate the vast centres of their overcrowded cities. Their large towns had no longer any large agricultural population from which to recruit their ranks, and through bad and insufficient food, vitiated atmosphere, and other insanitary conditions, the physique of the masses of the cities was rapidly deteriorating, both materially and physically.' Precisely; but does not Mr. Hyndman see that in striving to become possessed of present wealth forms, he is laying siege to the wrong fortress? If the population of London, or a large part of the population of London, is to be transplanted elsewhere, when some future event has happened, would it not be well to see if we cannot induce large numbers of these people to transplant themselves *now*, when the problem of London administration and of London reform would, as we shall shortly discover, present itself in a somewhat startling fashion?

A similar inconsistency is to be noticed in a little book which has had an enormous and well-deserved sale, *Merrie England*. The author, 'Nunquam',[1] remarks at the outset: 'The problem we have to consider is: Given a country and a people, find how the people may make the best of the country and themselves.' He then proceeds to vigorously condemn our cities, with their houses ugly and mean, their narrow streets, their want of gardens, and emphasizes the advantages of out-door occupations. He condemns the factory system, and says: 'I would set men to grow wheat and fruit, and rear cattle and poultry for our own use. Then I would develop the fisheries, and construct great fish-breeding lakes and harbours. Then I would restrict our mines, furnaces, chemical works, and factories to the number actually needed for the supply of our own people. Then I would stop the smoke nuisance by developing water-power and electricity. *In order to achieve these ends, I would make all the lands, mills, mines, factories, works, shops, ships, and railways the property of the people.*' That is (the italics are my own), the people are to struggle hard to become possessed of factories, mills, works and shops, at least half of which must be closed if Nunquam's desires are attained; of ships which will become useless if our foreign trade is to be abandoned (see *Merrie England*, Chap. IV); and of railways, which, with an entire redistribution of population such as Nunquam desires, must for the most part become derelict. And how long is this useless struggle to last? Would it

[1] Robert Blatchford.

not—I ask Nunquam to consider this point carefully—be better to study a smaller problem first, and, to paraphrase his words, 'Given, say, 6,000 acres of land, let us endeavour to make the best use of it'? For then, having dealt with this, we shall have educated ourselves to deal with a larger area.

Let me state again in other terms this fugitiveness of wealth forms, and then suggest the conclusion to which that consideration should lead us. So marked are the changes which society exhibits—especially a society in a progressive state—that the outward and visible forms which our civilization presents to-day, its public and private buildings, its means of communication, the appliances with which it works, its machinery, its docks, its artificial harbours, its instruments of war and its instruments of peace, have most of them undergone a complete change, and many of them several complete changes, within the last sixty years. I suppose not one person in twenty in this country is living in a house which is sixty years old; not one sailor in a thousand is sailing a ship, not one artisan or labourer in a hundred is engaged in a workshop or handling tools or driving a cart which was in existence sixty years ago. It is now sixty years since the first railway was constructed from Birmingham to London, and our Railway Companies possess one thousand millions of invested capital, while our systems of water supply, of gas, of electric lighting, and of sewerage are, for the most part, of recent date. Those material relics of the past which were created more than sixty years ago, though some of them are of infinite value as mementos, examples, and heirlooms, are, for the most part, certainly not of a kind which we need wrangle over or fight about. The best of them are our universities, schools, churches, and cathedrals, and these should certainly teach us a different lesson.

But can any reasonable person, who reflects for a moment on the recent unexampled rate of progress and invention, doubt that the next sixty years will reveal changes fully as remarkable? Can any person suppose that these mushroom forms, which have sprung up as it were in a night, have any real permanence? Even apart from the solution of the labour problem, and the finding of work for the thousands of idle hands which are eager for it—a solution, the correctness of which I claim to have demonstrated—what possibilities are opened up by the bare contemplation of the discovery of new motive powers, new means of locomotion, perhaps, through the air, new methods of water supply, or a new distribution of population, which must of itself render many material forms altogether useless and effete! Why, then, should we squabble and wrangle about what man *has* produced? Why not rather seek to learn what man *can* produce; when, aiming to do that, we may perhaps discover a grand opportunity for producing not only better forms of wealth, but how to produce them under far juster conditions? To quote the author of *Merrie England*: 'We should first of all ascertain what things are desirable for our health and happiness of body and mind, and then organize our people with the object of producing those things in the best and easiest way.'

Wealth forms, then, in their very nature are *fugitive*, and they are besides liable to constant displacement by the better forms which in an advancing state of society are constantly arising. There is, however, one form of material wealth which is most permanent and abiding; from the value and utility of which our most wonderful inventions can never detract one jot, but will serve only to make more clear, and to render more universal. The planet on which we live has lasted for millions of years, and the race is just emerging from its savagery. Those of us who believe that there is a grand purpose behind nature cannot believe that the career of this planet is likely to be speedily cut short now that better hopes are rising in the hearts of men, and that, having learned a few of its less obscure secrets, they are finding their way, through much toil and pain, to a more noble use of its infinite treasures. The earth for all practical purposes may be regarded as abiding for ever.

Now, as every form of wealth must rest on the earth as its foundation, and must be built up out of the constituents found at or near its surface, it follows (because foundations are ever of primary importance) that the reformer should first consider how best the earth may be used in the service of man. But here again our friends, the Socialists, miss the essential point. Their professed ideal is to make society the owner of land *and of all instruments of production*; but they have been so anxious to carry both points of their programme that they have been a little too slow to consider the special importance of the land question, and have thus missed the true path of reform.

There is, however, a type of reformers who push the land question very much to the front, though, as it appears to me, in a manner little likely to commend their views to society. Mr. Henry George, in his well-known work, *Progress and Poverty*, urges with much eloquence, if not with complete accuracy of reasoning, that our land laws are responsible for all the economic evils of society, and that as our landlords are little better than pirates and robbers, the sooner the State forcibly appropriates their rents the better, for when this is accomplished the problem of poverty will, he suggests, be entirely solved. But is not this attempt to throw the whole blame of and punishment for the present deplorable condition of society on to a single class of men a very great mistake? In what way are landlords as a class less honest than the average citizen? Give the average citizen the opportunity of becoming a landlord and of appropriating the land values created by his tenants, and he will embrace it to-morrow. If then, the average man is a potential landlord, to attack landlords as individuals is very like a nation drawing up an indictment against itself, and then making a scape-goat of a particular class.[1]

But to endeavour to change our land system is a very different matter from attacking those individuals who represent it. But how is this change to be effected? I reply: By the force of example, that is, by setting up a better system, and by a little skill in the grouping of forces and manipulation of ideas. It is quite true that the average man is a potential landlord, and as ready to appropriate the unearned increment as to cry out against its appropriation. But the average man has very little chance of ever becoming a landlord and of appropriating rent-values created by others; and he is, therefore, the better able to consider, quite dispassionately, whether such a proceeding is really honest, and whether it may not be possible to gradually establish a new and more equitable system under which, without enjoying the privilege of appropriating rent-values created by others, he may himself be secured against expropriation of the

[1] I hope it is not ungrateful in one who has derived much inspiration from *Progress and Poverty* to write thus.

rent-values which he is now constantly creating or maintaining. We have demonstrated how this may be done on a small scale; we have next to consider how the experiment may be carried out on a much wider scale, and this we can best do in another chapter.

Chapter Twelve

Social Cities

'Human nature will not flourish, any more than a potato, if it be planted and replanted for too long a series of generations in the same worn-out soil. My children have had other birthplaces, and, so far as their fortunes may be within my control, shall strike their roots into unaccustomed earth.'—NATHANIEL HAWTHORNE, *The Scarlet Letter*.

'The question which now interests people is, What are we going to do with democracy now that we have got it? What kind of society are we going to make by its aid? Are we to see nothing but an endless vista of Londons and Manchesters, New Yorks and Chicagos, with their noise and ugliness, their money-getting, their "corners" and "rings", their strikes, their contrasts of luxury and squalor? Or shall we be able to build up a society with art and culture for all, and with some great spiritual aim dominating men's lives?'—*Daily Chronicle*, 4th March 1891.

The problem with which we have now to deal, shortly stated, is this: How to make our Garden City experiment the stepping stone to a higher and better form of industrial life generally throughout the country. Granted the success of the initial experiment, and there must inevitably arise a widespread demand for an extension of methods so healthy and so advantageous; and it will be well, therefore, to consider some of the chief problems which will have to be faced in the progress of such extension.

It will, I think, be well, in approaching this question, to consider the analogy presented by the early progress of railway enterprise. This will help us to see more clearly some of the broader features of the new development which is now so closely upon us if only we show ourselves energetic and imaginative. Railways were first made without any statutory powers. They were constructed on a very small scale, and, being of very short lengths, the consent of only one or at the most a few landowners was necessary; and what private agreement and arrangement could thus easily compass was scarcely a fit subject for an appeal to the Legislature of the country. But when the 'Rocket' was built, and the supremacy of the locomotive was fully established, it then became necessary, if railway enterprise was to go forward, to obtain legislative powers. For it would have been impossible, or at least very difficult, to make equitable arrangements with all the landowners whose estates might lie between points many miles distant; because one obstinate landlord might take advantage of his position to demand an altogether exorbitant price for his land, and thus practically stifle such an enterprise. It was necessary, therefore, to obtain power to secure the land compulsorily at its market value, or at a price not too extravagantly removed from such value; and, this being done, railway enterprise went forward at so rapid a rate that in one year no less than £132,600,000 was authorized by Parliament to be raised for the purpose of railway construction.[1]

Now, if Parliamentary powers were necessary for the extension of railway enterprise, such powers will certainly be also needed when the inherent practicability of building new, well-planned towns, and of the population moving into them from the old slum cities as naturally as, and, in proportion to the power to be exercised, almost as easily as a family moves out of a rotten old tenement into a new and comfortable dwelling, is once fairly recognized by the people. To build such towns, large areas of land must be obtained. Here and there a suitable site may be secured by arrangement with one or more landowners, but if the movement is to be carried on in anything like a scientific fashion, stretches of land far larger than that occupied by our first experiment must be obtained. For, just as the first short railway, which was the germ of railway enterprise, would convey to few minds the conception of a network of railways extending over the whole country, so, perhaps, the idea of a well-planned town such as I have described will not have prepared the reader for the later development which must inevitably follow—the planning and building of town clusters—each town in the cluster being of different design from the others, and yet the whole forming part of one large and well-thought-out plan.

Let me here introduce a very rough diagram, representing, as

[1] Clifford's *History of Private Bill Legislation* (Butterworth, 1885), Introduction, p. 88.

I conceive, the true principle on which all towns should grow. Garden City has, we will suppose, grown until it has reached a population of 32,000. How shall it grow? How shall it provide for the needs of others who will be attracted by its numerous advantages? Shall it build on the zone of agricultural land which is around it, and thus for ever destroy its right to be called a 'Garden City'? Surely not. This disastrous result would indeed take place if the land around the town were, as is the land around our present cities, owned by private individuals anxious to make a profit out of it. For then, as the town filled up, the agricultural land would become 'ripe' for building purposes, and the beauty and healthfulness of the town would be quickly destroyed. But the land around Garden City is, fortunately, not in the hands of private individuals : it is in the hands of the people : and is to be administered, not in the supposed interests of the few, but in the real interests of the whole community. Now, there are few objects which the people so jealously guard as their parks and open spaces ; and we may, I think, feel confident that the people of Garden City will not for a moment permit the beauty of their city to be destroyed by the process of growth. But it may be urged—if this be true, will not the inhabitants of Garden City in this way be selfishly preventing the growth of their city, and thus preclude many from enjoying its advantages? Certainly not. There is a bright, but overlooked, alternative. The town *will* grow; but it will grow in accordance with a principle which will result in this—that such growth shall not lessen or destroy, but ever add to its social opportunities, to its beauty, to its convenience. Consider for a moment the case of a city in Australia which in some measure illustrates the principle for which I am contending. The city of Adelaide, as the accompanying sketch map shows, is surrounded by its 'Park Lands'. The city is built up. How does it grow? It grows by leaping over the 'Park Lands' and establishing North Adelaide.[1] And this is the

---

[1] Not only Adelaide, but a number of other cities in Australia and New Zealand, were originally planned with Park Belts. The inspiration of this practice has not been clearly traced, and is worth investigation. There are in history many other foreshadowings of Howard's idea of an inviolate zone of agricultural land around towns ; see, as examples, Leviticus 25, Ezekiel 35, and More's *Utopia* (1515). *Ed.*

Nº 4.

ADELAIDE

SHOWING PARK LANDS ALL ROUND
CITY, AND ITS MODE OF GROWTH.

NORTH PARK LANDS

PARK LANDS

STATION

WELLINGTON SQUARE

NORTH ADELAIDE

PARK LANDS

PARK LANDS

PARK LANDS

BOTANICAL GARDENS

RIVER TORRENS

STATION

NORWOOD

WEST PARK LANDS

LIGHT SQ.

HINDMARSH SQ.

ADELAIDE

VICTORIA SQ.

EAST PARK LANDS

WHITMORE SQ.

HURTLE SQ.

SOUTH PARK LANDS

ADELAIDE AND ITS LANDS

141

principle which it is intended to follow, but improve upon, in Garden City.

Our diagram may now be understood. Garden City is built up. Its population has reached 32,000. How will it grow? It will grow by establishing—under Parliamentary powers probably—another city some little distance beyond its own zone of 'country', so that the new town may have a zone of country of its own. I have said 'by establishing another city', and, for administrative purposes there would be *two* cities; but the inhabitants of the one could reach the other in a very few minutes; for rapid transit would be specially provided for, and thus the people of the two towns would in reality represent one community.

And this principle of growth—this principle of always preserving a belt of country round our cities would be ever kept in mind till, in course of time, we should have a cluster of cities, not of course arranged in the precise geometrical form of my diagram, but so grouped around a Central City that each inhabitant of the whole group, though in one sense living in a town of small size, would be in reality living in, and would enjoy all the advantages of, a great and most beautiful city; and yet all the fresh delights of the country—field, hedgerow, and woodland—not prim parks and gardens merely—would be within a very few minutes' walk or ride.[1] And *because the people in their collective capacity own the land* on which this beautiful group of cities is built, the public buildings, the churches, the schools and universities, the libraries, picture galleries, theatres, would be on a scale of magnificence which no city in the world whose land is in pawn to private individuals can afford.

[1] Professor Alfred Marshall, in his evidence to the Royal Commission on Imperial and Local Taxation (1899), suggested a national 'fresh air rate' as a means of securing country belts around and between towns: 'The central government should see to it that towns and industrial districts do not continue to increase without ample provision for that fresh air and wholesome play which are required to maintain the vigour of the people and their place among nations. . . . We need not only to widen our streets and increase the playgrounds in the midst of our towns. We need also to prevent one town from growing into another, or into a neighbouring village; we need to keep intermediate stretches of country in dairy farms, etc., as well as public pleasure grounds.' *Ed.*

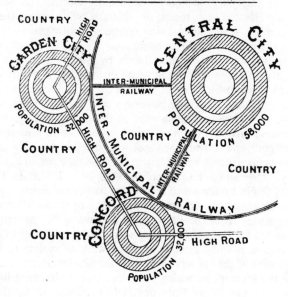

N⁰ 5.

— DIAGRAM —

ILLUSTRATING CORRECT PRINCIPLE
OF A CITY'S GROWTH – OPEN COUNTRY
EVER NEAR AT HAND, AND RAPID
COMMUNICATION BETWEEN OFF-SHOOTS.

COUNTRY

GARDEN CITY
HIGH ROAD

CENTRAL CITY

INTER-MUNICIPAL
RAILWAY

POPULATION 32,000

COUNTRY

COUNTRY

POPULATION 58,000

COUNTRY

INTER-MUNICIPAL HIGH ROAD

INTER-MUNICIPAL RAILWAY

COUNTRY

CONCORD

RAILWAY

POPULATION 32,000

HIGH ROAD

COUNTRY

CORRECT PRINCIPLE OF A CITY'S GROWTH

I have said that rapid railway transit would be realized by those who dwell in this beautiful city or group of cities. Reference to the diagram will show at a glance the main features of its railway system. There is, first, an inter-municipal railway, connecting all the towns of the outer ring—twenty miles in circumference—so that to get from any town to its most distant neighbour requires one to cover a distance of only ten miles, which could be accomplished in, say, twelve minutes. These trains would not stop between the towns—means of communication for this purpose being afforded by electric tramways which traverse the high roads, of which, it will be seen, there are a number—each town being connected with every other town in the group by a direct route.

There is also a system of railways by which each town is placed in direct communication with Central City. The distance from any town to the heart of Central City is only three and a quarter miles, and this could be readily covered in five minutes.

Those who have had experience of the difficulty of getting from one suburb of London to another will see in a moment what an enormous advantage those who dwell in such a group of cities as here shown would enjoy, because they would have a railway *system* and not a railway *chaos* to serve their ends. The difficulty felt in London is of course due to want of forethought and pre-arrangement. On this point, I may quote with advantage a passage from the Presidential address of Sir Benjamin Baker to the Institute of Civil Engineers, 12th November 1895: 'We Londoners often complain of the want of system in the arrangement of the railways and their terminal stations in and around the Metropolis, which necessitates our performing long journeys in cabs to get from one railway system to another. That this difficulty exists, arises, I feel sure, chiefly from the want of forethought of no less able a statesman than Sir Robert Peel, for, in 1836, a motion was proposed in the House of Commons that all the Railway Bills seeking powers for terminals in London should be referred to a Special Committee, so that a complete scheme might be evolved out of the numerous projects before Parliament, and that property might not be unnecessarily sacrificed for rival schemes. Sir Robert Peel opposed the motion on the part of the Government, on the grounds that "no railway project could come into operation till the majority of Parliament had declared that its principles and arrangements appeared to them satisfactory, and its investments profitable. It was a recognized principle in these cases that the probable profits of an undertaking should be shown to be sufficient to maintain it in a state of permanent utility before a Bill could be obtained, and landlords were perfectly justified in expecting and demanding such a warranty from Parliament." In this instance, incalculable injury was unintentionally inflicted upon Londoners by not having a grand central station in the Metropolis, and events have shown how false was the assumption that the passing of an Act implied any warranty as to the financial prospects of a railway.'

But are the people of England to suffer for ever for the want of foresight of those who little dreamed of the future development of railways? Surely not. It was in the nature of things little likely that the first network of railways ever constructed should conform to true principles; but now, seeing the enormous progress which has been made in the means of rapid communication, it is high time that we availed ourselves more fully of those means, and built our cities upon such some plan as that I have crudely shown. We should then be, for all purposes of quick communication, nearer to each other than we are in our crowded cities, while, at the same time, we should be surrounding ourselves with the most healthy and the most advantageous conditions.

Some of my friends have suggested that such a scheme of town clusters is well enough adapted to a new country, but that in an old-settled country, with its towns built, and its railway 'system' for the most part constructed, it is quite a different matter. But surely to raise such a point is to contend, in other words, that the existing wealth forms of the country are permanent, and are forever to serve as hindrances to the introduction of better forms: that crowded, ill-ventilated, unplanned, unwieldy, unhealthy cities—ulcers on the very face of our beautiful island—are to stand as barriers to the introduction of towns in which modern scientific methods and the aims of social reformers may have the fullest scope in which to express themselves. No, it cannot be; at least, it cannot be for long. What Is may hinder What Might Be for a while, but cannot stay the tide of progress. These crowded cities have done their work; they were the best which a society largely based on selfishness and rapacity could construct, but they are in the nature of things entirely unadapted for a society in which the social side of our nature is demanding a larger share of recognition—a society where even the very love of self leads us to insist upon a greater regard for the well-being of our fellows. The large cities of to-day are scarcely better adapted for the expression of the fraternal spirit than would a work on astronomy which taught that the earth was the centre of the universe be capable of adaptation for use in our schools. Each generation should build to suit its own needs; and it is no more in the nature of things that men should continue to live in old areas because their ancestors lived in them, than it is that they should cherish the old beliefs which a wider faith and a more enlarged understanding have outgrown. The reader is, therefore, earnestly asked not to take it for granted that the large cities in which he may perhaps take a pardonable pride are necessarily, in their present form, any more permanent than the stage-coach system which was the subject of so much admiration just at the very moment when it was about to be supplanted by the railways.[1] The simple issue to be faced, and faced resolutely, is: Can better results be obtained by starting on a bold plan on comparatively virgin soil than by attempting to adapt our old cities to our newer and higher needs? Thus fairly faced, the question can only be answered in one way; and when that simple fact is well grasped, the social revolution will speedily commence.

That there is ample land in this country on which such a cluster as I have here depicted could be constructed with *comparatively* small disturbance of vested interests, and, therefore, with but little need for compensation, will be obvious to anyone; and, when our first experiment has been brought to a successful issue, there will be no great difficulty in acquiring the necessary Parliamentary powers to purchase the land and carry out the necessary works step by step. County Councils are now seeking larger powers, and an overburdened Parliament is be-

[1] See, for instance, the opening chapter of *The Heart of Midlothian* (Sir Walter Scott).

146

coming more and more anxious to devolve some of its duties upon them. Let such powers be given more and more freely. Let larger and yet larger measures of local self-government be granted, and then all that my diagram depicts—only on a far better plan, because the result of well-concerted and combined thought—will be easily attainable.

But it may be said, 'Are you not, by thus frankly avowing the very great danger to the vested interests of this country which your scheme indirectly threatens, arming vested interests against yourself, and so making any change by legislation impossible?' I think not. And for three reasons. First, because those vested interests which are said to be ranged like a solid phalanx against progress, will, by the force of circumstances and the current of events, be for once divided into opposing camps. Secondly, because property owners, who are very reluctant to yield to threats, such as are sometimes made against them by Socialists of a certain type, will be far more ready to make concessions to the logic of events as revealing itself in an undoubted advance of society to a higher form; and, thirdly, because the largest and most important, and, in the end, the most influential of all vested interests—I mean the vested interests of those who work for their living, whether by hand or brain—will be naturally in favour of the change when they understand its nature.

Let me deal with these points separately. First, I say vested-property interests will be broken in twain, and will range themselves in opposite camps. This sort of cleavage has occurred before. Thus, in the early days of railway legislation, the vested interests in canals and stage coaches were alarmed, and did all in their power to thwart and hamper what threatened them. But other great vested interests brushed this opposition easily on one side. These interests were chiefly two—capital seeking investment, and land desiring to sell itself. (A third vested interest —namely, labour seeking employment—had then scarcely begun to assert its claims.) And notice now how such a successful experiment as Garden City may easily become will drive into the very bed-rock of vested interests a great wedge, which will split them asunder with irresistible force, and permit the current of legislation to set strongly in a new direction. For what will such an experiment have proved up to the very hilt? Among other things too numerous to mention, it will have proved that far more healthy and economic conditions can be secured on raw uncultivated land (if only that land be held on just conditions) than can be secured on land which is at present of vastly higher market value; and in proving this it will open wide the doors of migration from the old crowded cities with their inflated and artificial rents, back to the land which can be now secured so cheaply. Two tendencies will then display themselves. The first will be a strong tendency for city ground values to fall, the other a less marked tendency for agricultural land to rise.[1] The holders of agricultural land, at least those who are willing to sell—and many of them are even now most anxious to do so—will welcome the extension of an experiment which promises to place English agriculture once again in a position of prosperity: the holders of city lands will, so far as their merely selfish interests prevail, greatly fear it. In this way, landowners throughout the country will be divided into two opposing factions, and the path of land reform—the foundation on which all other reforms must be built—will be made comparatively easy.

Capital in the same way will be divided into opposite camps. Invested capital—that is, capital sunk in enterprises which society will recognize as belonging to the old order—will take the alarm and fall in value enormously, while, on the other hand, capital seeking investment will welcome an outlet which has long been its sorest need. Invested capital will in its opposition be further weakened by another consideration. Holders of existing forms of capital will strive—even though it be at a great sacrifice—to sell part of their old time-honoured stocks, and invest them in new enterprises, on municipally owned land, for they will not wish to 'have all their eggs in one basket'; and thus will the opposing influences of vested property neutralize each other.

But vested-property interests will be, as I believe, affected yet more remarkably in another way. The man of wealth, when he is personally attacked and denounced as an enemy of society, is slow to believe in the perfect good faith of those who denounce

[1] The chief reason for this is that agricultural land as compared with city land is of vastly larger quantity.

him, and, when efforts are made to tax him out by the forcible hand of the State, he is apt to use every endeavour, lawful or unlawful, to oppose such efforts, and often with no small measure of success. But the average wealthy man is no more an unmixed compound of selfishness than the average poor man; and if he sees his houses or lands depreciated in value, not by force, but because those who lived in or upon them have learned how to erect far better homes of their own, and on land held on conditions more advantageous to them, and to surround their children with many advantages which cannot be enjoyed on his estate, he will philosophically bow to the inevitable, and, in his better moments, even welcome a change which will involve him in far greater pecuniary loss than any change in the incidence of taxation is likely to inflict. In every man there is some measure of the reforming instinct; in every man there is some regard for his fellows; and when these natural feelings run athwart his pecuniary interests, then the result is that the spirit of opposition is inevitably softened, in some degree in all men, while in others it is entirely replaced by a fervent desire for the country's good, even at the sacrifice of many cherished possessions. Thus it is that what will not be yielded to a force from without may readily be granted as the result of an impulse from within.

And now let me deal for a moment with the greatest, the most valuable, and the most permanent of all vested interests—the vested interests of skill, labour, energy, talent, industry. How will these be affected? My answer is, the force which will divide in twain the vested interests of land and capital will unite and consolidate the interests of those who live by work, and will lead them to unite their forces with the holders of agricultural land and of capital seeking investment, to urge upon the State the necessity for the prompt opening up of facilities for the reconstruction of society; and, when the State is slow to act, then to employ voluntary collective efforts similar to those adopted in the Garden City experiment, with such modifications as experience may show to be necessary. Such a task as the construction of a cluster of cities like that represented in our diagram may well inspire all workers with that enthusiasm which unites men, for it will call for the very highest talents of engineers of all kinds, of architects, artists, medical men, experts in sanitation, landscape gardeners, agricultural experts, surveyors, builders, manufacturers, merchants and financiers, organizers of trades unions, friendly and co-operative societies, as well as the very simplest forms of unskilled labour, together with all those forms of lesser skill and talent which lie between. For the vastness of the task which seems to frighten some of my friends, represents, in fact, the very measure of its value to the community, if that task be only undertaken in a worthy spirit and with worthy aims. Work in abundance is, as has been several times urged, one of the greatest needs of to-day, and no such field of employment has been opened up since civilization began as would be represented by the task which is before us of reconstructing anew the entire external fabric of society, employing, as we build, all the skill and knowledge which the experience of centuries has taught us. It was 'a large order' which was presented in the early part of this century to construct iron highways throughout the length and breadth of this island, uniting in a vast network all its towns and cities. But railway enterprise, vast as has been its influence, touched the life of the people at but few points compared with the newer call to build home-towns for slum cities; to plant gardens for crowded courts; to construct beautiful water-ways in flooded valleys; to establish a scientific system of distribution to take the place of a chaos, a just system of land tenure for one representing the selfishness which we hope is passing away; to found pensions with liberty for our aged poor, now imprisoned in workhouses; to banish despair and awaken hope in the breasts of those who have fallen; to silence the harsh voice of anger, and to awaken the soft notes of brotherliness and goodwill; to place in strong hands implements of peace and construction, so that implements of war and destruction may drop uselessly down. Here is a task which may well unite a vast army of workers to utilize that power, the present waste of which is the source of half our poverty, disease, and suffering.

Chapter Thirteen

The Future of London

It will now be interesting to consider some of the more striking effects which will be produced on our now overcrowded cities by the opening up in new districts of such a vast field of employment as the reader's mind will, it is hoped, be now able to realize with some degree of clearness. New towns and groups of towns are springing up in parts of our islands hitherto wellnigh deserted; new means of communication, the most scientific the world has yet seen, are being constructed; new means of distribution are bringing the producer and the consumer into closer relations, and thus (by reducing railway rates and charges, and the number of profits) are at once raising prices to the producer and diminishing them to the consumer; parks and gardens, orchards and woods, are being planted in the midst of the busy life of the people, so that they may be enjoyed in the fullest measure; homes are being erected for those who have long lived in slums; work is found for the workless, land for the landless, and opportunities for the expenditure of long pent-up energy are presenting themselves at every turn. A new sense of freedom and joy is pervading the hearts of the people as their individual faculties are awakened, and they discover, in a social life which permits alike of the completest concerted action and of the fullest individual liberty, the long-sought-for means of reconciliation between order and freedom—between the well-being of the individual and of society.

The effects produced on our over-crowded cities, whose forms are at once, by the light of a new contrast, seen to be old-fashioned and effete, will be so far-reaching in their character that, in order to study them effectively, it will be well to confine our attention to London, which, as the largest and most unwieldy of our cities, is likely to exhibit those effects in the most marked degree.

There is, as I said at the outset, a wellnigh universal current of opinion that a remedy for the depopulation of our country districts and for the overcrowding of our large cities is urgently needed. But though everyone recommends that a remedy should be diligently sought for, few appear to believe that such a remedy will ever be found, and the calculations of our statesmen and reformers proceed upon the assumption that not only will the tide of population never actually turn from the large cities countryward, but that it will continue to flow in its present direction at a scarcely diminished rate for a long time to come.[1] Now it can hardly be supposed that any search made in the full belief that the remedy sought for will not be discovered is likely to be carried on with great zeal or thoroughness; and therefore, it is perhaps not surprising to find that though the late chairman of the London County Council (Lord Rosebery) declared that the growth of this huge city was fitly comparable to the growth of a tumour (see p. 42)—few venturing to deny the correctness of the analogy—yet the various members of that body, instead of bending their energies to reforming London by means of a reduction of its population, are boldly advocating a policy which involves the purchase of vast undertakings on behalf of the municipality, at prices which must prove far higher than they will be worth if only the long-sought-for remedy is found.

Let us now assume (simply as an hypothesis, if the reader is still sceptical) that the remedy advocated in this work is effective; that new garden cities are springing up all over the country on sites owned by the municipalities—the rate-rents of such corporate property forming a fund ample for the carrying on of municipal undertakings representing the highest skill of the modern engineer and the best aspirations of the enlightened re-

---

[1] It is scarcely necessary to give instances of what is meant; but one that occurs to my mind is that this assumption of the continued growth of London forms one of the fundamental premises of the Report of the Royal Commission on Metropolitan Water Supply, 1893. On the contrary, it is satisfactory to note that Mr. H. G. Wells has recently entirely changed his views as to the future growth of London. (see *Anticipations*, Chap. ii). Read also 'The Distribution of Industry', by P. W. Wilson, in *The Heart of the Empire* (Fisher Unwin), and Paper by Mr. W. L. Madgen, M.I.E.E., on 'Industrial Redistribution', *Society of Arts Journal*, February 1902.

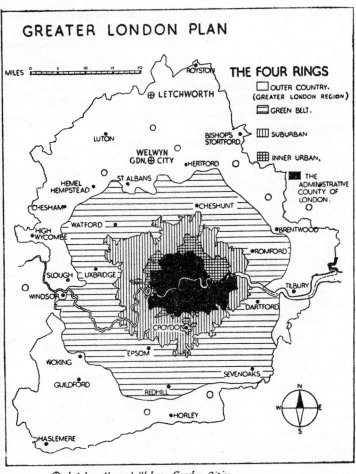

⊕ Letchworth and Welwyn Garden Cities
○ Proposed sites for new "satellite" towns in Plan

THE GARDEN CITY IDEA APPLIED TO LONDON. PROPOSED SITING OF EIGHT TO TEN NEW SATELLITE TOWNS AND RESERVATION OF COUNTRY BELT IN PROFESSOR SIR PATRICK ABERCROMBIE'S GREATER LONDON PLAN 1944 former; and that in these cities, healthier, wholesomer, cleaner and more just and sound economic conditions prevail. What, then, must in the nature of things be the more noticeable effects upon London and the population of London; upon its land values; upon its municipal debt, and its municipal assets; upon London as a labour market; upon the homes of its people; upon its open spaces, and upon the great undertakings which our socialistic and municipal reformers are at the present moment so anxious to secure?

First, notice that ground values will fall enormously! Of course, so long as the 121 square miles out of the 58,000 square miles of England exercise a magnetic attraction so great as to draw to it one-fifth of the whole population, who compete fiercely with each other for the right to occupy the land within that small area, so long will that land have a monopoly price. But de-magnetize that people, convince large numbers of them that they can better their condition in every way by migrating elsewhere, and what becomes of that monopoly value? Its spell is broken, and the great bubble bursts.

But the life and earnings of Londoners are not only in pawn to the owners of its soil, who kindly permit them to live upon it at enormous rents—£16,000,000 per annum, representing the present ground value of London, which is yearly increasing; but they are also in pawn to the extent of about £40,000,000, representing London's municipal debts.

But notice this. A municipal debtor is quite different from an ordinary debtor in one most important respect. *He can escape payment by migration.* He has but to move away from a given municipal area, and he at once, *ipso facto*, shakes off not only all his obligations to his landlord, but also all his obligations to his municipal creditors. It is true, when he migrates he must assume the burden of a new municipal rent, and of a new municipal debt; but these in our new cities will represent an extremely small and diminishing fraction of the burden now borne, and the temptation to migrate will, for this and many other reasons, be extremely strong.

But now let us notice how each person in migrating from London, while making the burden of *ground-rents* less heavy for those who remain, will (unless there be some change in the law), make the burden of *rates* on the ratepayers of London yet heavier. For, though each person in migrating will enable those who remain to make better and yet better terms with their landlords; on the other hand, the municipal debt remaining the same, the interest on it will have to be borne by fewer and yet fewer people, and thus the relief to the working population which comes from *reduced rent* will be largely discounted by *increased rates,* and in this way the temptation to migrate will continue, and yet further population will remove, making the debt ever a larger and larger burden, till at length, though accompanied by a still further reduction of rent, it may become intolerable. Of course this huge debt need never have been incurred. Had London been built on municipally-owned land, its rents would not only have easily provided for all current expenditure, without any need for a levy of rates or for incurring loans for long periods, but it would have been enabled to own its own water-supply and many other useful and profit-bearing undertakings, instead of being in its present position with vast debts and small assets. But a vicious and immoral system is bound ultimately to snap, and when the breaking-point is reached, the owners of London's bonds will, like the owners of London's land, have to make terms with a people who can apply the simple remedy of migrating and building a better and brighter civilization elsewhere, if they are not allowed to rebuild on a just and reasonable basis on the site of their ancient city.

We may next notice, very briefly, the bearing of this migration of population upon two great problems—the problem of the housing of the people of London, and the problem of finding employment for those who remain. The rents now paid by the working population of London, for accommodation most miserable and insufficient, represents each year a larger and larger proportion of income, while the cost of moving to and from work, continually increasing, often represents in time and money a very considerable tax. But imagine the population of London falling, and falling rapidly; the migrating people establishing themselves where rents are extremely low, and where their work is within easy walking distance of their homes! Obviously, house-property in London will fall in rental value, and fall enormously. Slum property will sink to zero, and the whole working population will move into houses of a class quite above those which they can now afford to occupy. Families which are now compelled to huddle together in one room will be able to rent five or six, and thus will the housing problem temporarily solve itself by the simple process of a diminution in the numbers of the tenants.

But what will become of this slum property? Its power to extort a large proportion of the hard earnings of the London poor gone for ever, will it yet remain an eye-sore and a blot, though no longer a danger to health and an outrage on decency? No. These wretched slums will be pulled down, and their sites occupied by parks, recreation grounds, and allotment gardens. And this change, as well as many others, will be effected, not at the expense of the ratepayers, but almost entirely at the expense of the landlord class: in this sense, at least, that such ground rents as are still paid by the people of London in respect of those classes of property which retain some rental value will have to bear the burden of improving the city. Nor will, I think, the compulsion of any Act of Parliament be necessary to effect this result: it will probably be achieved by the voluntary action of the landowners, compelled, by a Nemesis from whom there is no escape, to make some restitution for the great injustice which they have so long committed.

For observe what must inevitably happen. A vast field of employment being opened outside London, unless a corresponding field of employment is opened within it, London must die—when the landowners will be in a sorry plight. Elsewhere new cities are being built: London then must be transformed. Elsewhere the town is invading the country: here the country must invade the town. Elsewhere cities are being built on the terms of paying low prices for land, and of then vesting such land in the new municipalities: in London corresponding arrangements must be made or no one will consent to build. Elsewhere, owing to the fact that there are but few interests to buy out, improvements of all kinds can go forward rapidly and scientifically: in London similar improvements can only be carried out if vested interests recognize the inevitable and accept terms which may seem ridiculous, but are no more so than those which a manufacturer often finds himself compelled to submit to, who sells for a ridiculously low price the machine which has cost a very large sum, for the simple reason that there is a far better one in the market, and that it no longer *pays*, in the face of keen competition, to work the inferior machine. The displacement of capital will, no doubt, be enormous but the implacement of labour will be yet greater. A few may be made comparatively poor, but the many will be made comparatively rich—a very healthy change, the slight evils attending which society will be well able to mitigate.

There are already visible symptoms of the coming change— rumblings which precede the earthquake. London at this very moment may be said to be on strike against its landowners. Long-desired London improvements are awaiting such a change in the law as will throw some of the cost of making them upon the landowners of London. Railways are projected, but in some cases are not built—for instance, The Epping Forest Railway —because the London County Council, most properly anxious to keep down the fares by workmen's trains, press for and secure, at the hands of a Parliamentary Committee, the imposition of terms upon the promoters which seem to them extremely onerous and unremunerative, but which would pay the company extremely well were it not for the prohibitive price asked for land and other property along the line of its projected route. These checks upon enterprise must affect the growth of London even now, and make it less rapid than it otherwise would be; but when the untold treasures of our land are unlocked, and when the people now living in London discover how easily vested interests, without being attacked, may be circumvented, then the landowners of London and those who represent other vested interests had better quickly make terms, or London, besides being what Mr. Grant Allen termed 'a squalid village', will also become a deserted one.

But better counsels, let us hope, will prevail, and a new city rise on the ashes of the old. The task will indeed be difficult. Easy, comparatively, is it to lay out on virgin soil the plan of a magnificent city, such as represented on our Diagram 5. Of far greater difficulty is the problem—even if all vested interests freely effaced themselves—of rebuilding a new city on an old site, and that site occupied by a huge population. But this, at least, is certain, that the present area of the London County Council ought not (if health and beauty, and that which is too frequently put in the front rank—rapid production of wealth forms—are to be considered) to contain more than, say, one-fifth of its present population; and that new systems of railways, sewerage, drainage, lighting, parks, etc., must be constructed if London is to be saved, while the whole system of production and of distribution must undergo changes as complete and as remarkable as was the change from a system of barter to our present complicated commercial system.

Proposals for the reconstruction of London have already been projected. In 1883 the late Mr. William Westgarth offered the Society of Arts the sum of £1,200 to be awarded in prizes for essays on the best means of providing dwellings for the London poor, and on the reconstruction of Central London—an offer which brought forward several schemes of some boldness.[1] More recently a book by Mr. Arthur Cawston, entitled *A Comprehensive Scheme for Street Improvements in London*, was published by Stanford, which contains in its introduction the following striking passage: 'The literature relating to London, extensive as it is, contains no work which aims at the solution of one problem of vast interest to Londoners. They are beginning to realize, partly by their more and more extensive travels, and partly through their American and foreign critics, that the gigantic growth of their capital, without the controlling guidance of a municipality, has resulted in not only the biggest, but in probably the most irregular, inconvenient, and unmethodical collection of houses in the world. A comprehensive plan for the transformation of Paris has been gradually developed since 1848; slums have disappeared from Berlin since 1870; eighty-eight acres in the centre of Glasgow have been remodelled; Birmingham has transformed ninety-three acres of squalid slums into magnificent streets flanked by architectural buildings; Vienna, having completed her stately outer ring, is about to remodel her inner city: and the aim of the writer is to show, by example and illustration, in what way the means successfully employed for improving these cities can be best adapted to the needs of London.'

[1] See *Reconstruction of Central London* (George Bell and Sons).

THE FUTURE OF LONDON

The time for the complete reconstruction of London—which will eventually take place on a far more comprehensive scale than that now exhibited in Paris, Berlin, Glasgow, Birmingham, or Vienna—has, however, not yet come. A simpler problem must first be solved. One small Garden City must be built as a working model, and then a group of cities such as that dealt with in the last chapter. These tasks done, and done well, the reconstruction of London must inevitably follow, and the power of vested interests to block the way will have been almost, if not entirely, removed.

Let us, therefore, first bend all our energies to the smaller of these tasks, thinking only of the larger tasks which lie beyond as incentives to a determined line of immediate action, and as a means of realizing the great value of little things if done in the right manner and in the right spirit.

THE END

A Select Book List

There is a vast literature of books, pamphlets and articles in periodicals dealing with the Garden City movement (rightly and wrongly understood), but relatively few of these make important contributions to the subject. The following is a selection of those having historic or current interest.

Abercrombie, Patrick, *Greater London Plan* 1944 (H.M. Stationery Office, London. Public issue 1945). Immense advance on all previous plans for metropolitan regions. Based on conceptions of community planning, and of relation of town and country, clearly derived from Howard's proposals.

Benoit-Levy, Georges, *La Cité-Jardin*, Preface by Charles Gide (Paris 1904). One of the earliest of innumerable foreign books on the Garden City movement. Like many others, confuses the Garden City with the Open Suburb.

Barlow Report, *Report of Royal Commission on Distribution of Industrial Population* (H.M. Stationery Office, London 1940). Recommends national planning, limitation of size of cities, dispersal to smaller towns, and governmental guidance of location of industry. A turning point in British town planning.

Howard, Ebenezer, *Domestic Industry as it Might Be* (Pamphlet, London 1906). Expands the hint of co-operative housekeeping in his book. Howard inspired two experiments in this field at Letchworth.

McAllister, G. and E., *Town and Country Planning* (Faber and Faber, 1941). Relates recent history of British housing to the Garden City idea.

Macfadyen, Dugald, *Sir Ebenezer Howard and the Garden City Movement* (Manchester University Press, 1933). Somewhat informally arranged, but contains all essential facts about Howard, and many interesting personal impressions.

Ministry of Housing and Local Government, *South East Study* (London, 1964). Proposals for dispersal and regional development, including further new towns.

A SELECT BOOK LIST

Marley Report, *Report of Departmental Committee on Garden Cities* (H.M. Stationery Office, London 1935). Advocates the establishment of Garden Cities and of a national Planning Board to influence location of industry therein. No action was taken on this report.

Mumford, Lewis, *The Culture of Cities* (New York and London, 1938). Profound study, sociological and historical, of inter-action of urban environment and human personality. Contains one of the best modern evaluations of Ebenezer Howard's ideas. Also a superb bibliography—omitted in second London edition.
The City in History (New York and London, 1961). Carries further the analysis and philosophical study of urban development from its beginnings. Again endorses Howard's thesis.

New Towns Committee, *First, Second, and Final Reports* (H.M. Stationery Office, London, 1946). Compact prescriptions for every aspect of new town development.

New Town Development Corporations, *Reports*, annual (London and Edinburgh, 1948 to date). Full progress reports and accounts for new towns in England and Wales, and Scotland.

National Resources Board (U.S.), *Our Cities: Their Role in the National Economy* (Washington 1937). Fascinating study of character and statistics of American cities, including problem of size and distribution.
Urban Planning and Land Policies (Washington 1941). Includes valuable record of a large number of deliberately founded towns and communities in U.S.

Osborn, F. J., and Whittick, A., *The New Towns: The Answer to Megalopolis* (London and New York, 1963). Account of the first 19 British New Towns, with plans and photographs, history of evolution of policy, and critique of antagonisms.

Osborn, F. J., *New Towns after the War* (London, 1918 and 1942). A short re-statement of Garden City principles. The story of Howard's foundation of Welwyn Garden City is told in the 1942 Preface.
Transport, Town Development, and the Territorial Planning of Industry (London, 1934). Critique of metropolitan structure and proposals for governmental guidance of location of industry as a means of controlling size and distribution of towns.

A SELECT BOOK LIST

Purdom, C. B., *The Garden City* (London 1913).
  The Building of Satellite Towns (London, 1925 and 1949). The former book is an intimate account of the foundation and early development of Letchworth. The latter, better documented, deals fully with Letchworth and Welwyn Garden City up to 1949.
  (ed.), *Town Theory and Practice* (London, 1921). Symposium by various writers, including important chapter by Sir Raymond Unwin foreshadowing his Regional Plan for London.
  The Letchworth Achievement (London, 1963). Describes how the danger of the commercialization of the First Garden City was averted by public acquisition in 1962.

Rosner, Rolf, *Neue Städte in England* (Munich, 1962, German text). Intelligently critical and handsomely illustrated.

Saarinen, Eliel, *The City: its Growth, its Decay, its Future* (New York, 1943). Interesting as an architect's reconciliation of the aesthetic and human approaches to urban planning. Resultant pattern is very close to Howard's *Social Cities*.

Scott Report, *Report of Committee on Land Utilization in Rural Areas* (H.M. Stationery Office, London 1942). Primarily concerned with safeguards for agriculture and countryside interests in applying Barlow Report policy of industrial dispersal.

Self, Peter, *Cities in Flood* (London, 1957 and 1961). First-class study of the metropolitan problem, with well-thought-out proposals.

Stein, Clarence, *Toward New Towns for America* (Liverpool, 1951). Fully illustrated and documented account of Radburn, Greenbelt Towns and other planned communities in USA.

Town and Country Planning Association (then Garden Cities and Town Planning Association), *Evidence to Barlow Royal Commission* (London 1938). Relates Garden City thesis to national planning policy. Influenced findings of Commission.

Town and Country Planning Association, *The Paper Metropolis* (London, 1961). This and the many earlier and later publications of the TCPA have led planning thought in Britain.

Towndrow, F. E. (ed.), *Replanning Britain* (Faber and Faber, 1941). Report of 1941 Conference at Oxford which did much to crystallize current British planning policy.

Tyerman, D. (ed.), *Country Towns in a Future England* (Faber and Faber, 1944). Beginning of a collective assertion by British country towns of their claims *vis-a-vis* the great cities.

Unwin, Raymond, *Nothing Gained by Overcrowding* (T. & C.P. Assn., London, 1912). Classic statement of case for low-density housing, an essential component of good planning and therefore of good Garden City planning, but not to be confused with the Garden City idea itself.

Greater London Regional Planning Reports (London, 1929 and 1933). Basically sound and historically important, but neglected by the authorities. Now superseded by Abercrombie Report of 1944.

Uthwatt Report, *Report of Expert Committee on Compensation and Betterment* (H.M. Stationery Office, London 1942). Masterly analysis of problem of increases and reductions of land values involved in dispersal planning and shifts of population, with logical but highly contentious recommendations. Indispensible to study of modern urban problem.

Viet, Jean, *Les Villes Nouvelles* (*New Towns*) (Unesco, 1960). Bibliography of 790 publications in many countries. Now needs supplementation, but most useful.

Warren, Herbert, and Davidge, W. R., *Decentralization of Population and Industry* (London, 1930). Symposium with chapters of uneven value.

For the history of the Garden City movement, the richest source is the file of the Association journal, successively named *The Garden City*, *Garden Cities and Town Planning*, and *Town and Country Planning* (London 1904 to date).

To-Morrow: A Peaceful Path to Real Reform was published in 1898. The second edition, renamed *Garden Cities of To-morrow*, appeared in 1902, slightly revised and with a Postscript by the Author. A third edition was issued in 1922, with a Foreword by Sir Theodore Chambers, K.B.E.

Translations have been published in French, Russian, Czech, and Italian, and there are summaries in books by writers in other languages.

Index